ROWING
AND SCULLING

ROWING AND SCULLING

The Complete Manual

BILL SAYER

THIRD EDITION

ROBERT HALE · LONDON

© Bill Sayer 1991, 1996, 2006 & 2013
First published in Great Britain 1991
New and expanded edition 2006
Third edition 2013

ISBN 978-0-7198-0989-7

Robert Hale Limited
Clerkenwell House
Clerkenwell Green
London EC1R 0HT

www.halebooks.com

A catalogue record for this book is available from the British Library

10 9 8 7 6 5 4 3 2

Typeset by e-type, Liverpool
Printed in India

Contents

Acknowledgements

I would like to thank all my fellow coaches who helped to shape my own rowing and sculling career and who also shared their expertise and friendship. I was very fortunate to have had the pleasure of coaching and guiding a very large number of young athletes. We had a lot of fun and I am very grateful to them and especially those who wittingly or not appear in the illustrations. Without them and what I learnt from them there would be no book.

My wife Margaret, a very fine coach in her own right, has been a staunch supporter and essential help throughout my years of coaching and in the preparation of this book.

I am indebted to Robert Hale Limited for their skill and faith in the project from its raw beginnings through to this splendid edition.

Introduction

This new paperback edition of the book has been further updated and revised to take account of the many ways in which our sport has moved forward. The London Olympics demonstrated a huge measure of success for the superbly organised Team GB; it was also apparent that very similar technical principles and training methods are now being used in the majority of countries. This book seeks to explain these principles and methods so that readers, whatever their present level of performance, can further enhance their successful enjoyment of the sport.

In 1990 the Berlin wall fell and the secrets of the East German domination of world rowing began to become more transparent. Some of their methods were reprehensible but those of us who were involved in international rowing at the time had long admired their thorough and effective preparation. Former DDR coaches have moved on to be very successful elsewhere but in many countries the application of science has enabled training to become more effective and equipment to improve. Better financial support for aspiring athletes and the proven performers and a changed attitude to professionalism has enabled many more to train at a level which was formerly common only for those with state support.

Boats have not changed a lot in design in recent years but their construction has been refined. Oars and sculls, however, are now very different to those in use when the book first came out. Juniors and women now race the full 2,000 metres in major regattas and training methods for both them and senior men have changed considerably in emphasis. These changes reflect both the contribution of scientific research and the successful experience of the competitors using the new approaches. As a result, the times over standard courses continue to fall and it is clear from the trend that further improvements can be expected.

As in the earlier editions, I have tried to survey the whole of the complex of factors that make a rowing boat go fast. This book will

introduce you to the technical skills that you need and help you to
improve them. It will show you how to plan your training to get the
most from your body and how to get the most from your equipment.
Later chapters will inform you how to race most effectively and, lastly,
it will guide you in how to look after yourself so that you are not
hampered by avoidable hazards and can make the most of your body's
capabilities.

I trust that you will find this new book as helpful as many people
found the earlier one in your search for greater sporting success and
pleasure. You need some good luck as well, but as the great golfer Gary
Player said, 'The harder I try, the luckier I get.' So try hard, use the
information, and make your own luck!

1 Rowing and Sculling – An Introduction to the Sports

There is both archaeological and documentary evidence to show that boats have been sculled or rowed, with oars forced against a fixed part of the boat, for many millennia and doubtless early man raced his friends in his coracle or dugout. We know that the classical civilizations had formalized crew rowing races and it is not hard to imagine that competition in rowing boats goes back very much further. All over the world there are races for rowing and sculling boats which are long-established and show our need to compare and test ourselves against others. Such competitive sports reflected the importance of the rowing boat for transport, and even for war, and were commonly seen as a way of enhancing performance for adults, and developing children's skill and physique for more serious purposes. For some events very valuable prizes were given, large wagers were exchanged and the crowds bet prodigious sums on the results.

Particularly in the nineteenth century a tradition began to build of sporting challenges between 'gentlemen', purely for fun and without money at stake. Thus arose the idea of the 'amateur', who might well hire a professional waterman as coach but would exclude him from the competition. Unfortunately this meant that the history of the sport was marked until relatively recently by a very snobbish attitude which sought to exclude the working man and those 'in trade', and also greatly restricted women's rowing. The result was a definition of 'amateur' that limited competition in domestic regattas and even international events to a self-chosen elite, and would even disqualify those who dared to row with or against the labouring classes. Thankfully all that has gone and both clubs and competitions are open to all those who qualify by age or experience.

Fig. 1 British school rowing at its best – the excitement of multi-lane racing in the National Schools Regatta in Nottingham

JOINING A CLUB

In order to take part in open competition it is necessary to belong to a club which is affiliated to the national federation (in Britain this is British Rowing (BR)), and each member will need to be registered. This brings many other advantages such as insurance cover and access to the expertise of the federation, and in any case most people will want to be sociable and enjoy the benefits of club membership. Apart from the social aspects of club life there are the undoubted advantages of crew rowing or sculling, and of having an administrative, coaching and financial organization. The majority of readers will row or scull as members of such a club, whether it is part of their school or university sports facilities, or independent. At the top level of the sport athletes will seek out a club which can provide them with the best facilities and equipment, inspiring coaches and enough like-minded fellow athletes to form worthwhile crews. Many of the best athletes will compete in composites of several feeder clubs or under a flag of convenience.

Fig. 2 Rowing with your friends in a club or school crew is very rewarding

If you are not already a member of a club then you can probably find a local one most easily through your phone book or by contacting your national federation. In my experience they have always been most helpful and welcoming, and if you are away from home why not make contact with the local club and meet some like-minded people?

SAFETY

Clubs and the administrative organization (such as BR) are also responsible for issuing and implementing advice on water safety and the club will have a safety officer. The club and its members will be regularly assessed on their adherence to the safety rules. It is essential that you are fully conversant with the latest safety regulations and essential for everyone's safety as well as your own that you adhere strictly to them. Rowing is a safe sport, but as with any water sport, there are particular hazards, and perhaps we are at particular risk because we travel rather fast and we are not looking where we are going most of the time. Reference to safety matters is made in various sections of this book, but in particular it is essential that you are able to swim well before you even think of going afloat. Not only must you be able to swim well, but you must also be confident, so that if you are suddenly pitched into freezing water on a dark night you do not panic, but know what to do.

Rowing tends to breed tough-mindedness and we become used to training in unpleasant conditions – but don't let an excess of enthusiasm take you out in unsafe conditions when prudence dictates otherwise. Unless you are very sure, always seek experienced advice, and still be prepared to err on the side of caution if you are still in doubt. Blanket rules can never be entirely adequate; you must do all you can to learn the special hazards of your stretch of water and to understand its changes.

TYPES OF COMPETITION

Worldwide the sport continues to grow both in terms of total numbers participating and in the range of competitions available. Now that rowing machines (ergometers) are commonplace and reliable there are increasing numbers of indoor competitions and even world championships, and many of the competitors will never have sat in a boat. Whether on or off the water there are opportunities for practically all age groups, both sexes and the disabled. In addition many events are further divided on the basis of experience or past successes. The provision of lightweight classes for both men and women has become increasingly popular and recognizes that ultimately there is an advantage to those who are significantly above average in height and weight.

The professional races of centuries past took place over a range of distances on many bodies of water – for example half-a-mile on the River Tyne or from Westminster to Hammersmith on the Tideway. Although there were rowing races at Oxford and Cambridge Universities by the early nineteenth century, the first race between the two was in 1829 on the Thames at Henley. The Boat Race, as it came to be known, was held again in 1836 from Westminster to Putney (then the championship course for professionals) and in 1845 the Putney to Mortlake distance was adopted and has been retained ever since. This course is also now used, but in the opposite direction, for the most famous of the long-distance, timed processional head-of-the-river races. Regattas for side by side or handicap races vary from 500-metre 'sprint' events to the international distance of 2,000 metres or more (Henley Royal is about 2,100m). There are even some much longer 'marathon' events such as the 31-mile Lincoln to Boston Marathon, or the Tour de Lac Leman. Since competition can be found for all types of boat from single sculls to eights, there is room in the sport for everyone, from the young beginner to the octogenarian, to measure themselves against their peers, to try to improve their own standards, or simply to enjoy taking part.

In each country the national rowing federation publishes its own rules for domestic competition, and in Great Britain these are found in the indispensable annual *British Rowing Almanack* published by BR. The various national federations are affiliated to the Fédération Internationale des Sociétés d'Aviron (FISA), which is the governing body for international rowing and sculling competition and which issues the rules applicable to such events. Many of the domestic rules are based on those of FISA, although there are some significant differences, and in both cases the intending competitor must beware of the frequent amendments. A summary of the principal categories of events under FISA rules is given in Table 1.

Table 1   FISA racing classes

1 **Junior**   Not attained age 18 before 1st January of the current year.
2 **Senior A**   Open to all competitors.
3 **Senior B**   Not attained age 23 before 1st January.
4 **Lightweight men**   Maximum weight for a rower or sculler is 72.5 kg, but the average weight for a crew shall not exceed 70 kg (excluding cox).
5 **Lightweight women**   Maximum weight for a rower or sculler is 59 kg, but the average weight for a crew shall not exceed 57 kg.
6 **Veteran/Masters**   27 years or older in the current year. Further categories are as follows for the average age of crews (excluding cox), or for single scullers attaining that age during the current year:
   A - Open to any veteran; **B** 36; **C** 43; **D** 50; **E** 55; **F** 60; **G** 65; **H** 70.
7 **Coxes**   The rules concerning Juniors apply also to coxes, but for other events the cox is not classified. Different minimum weight rules for Junior, Men's and Women's crews apply, and there are also rules concerning dead weight carried by the cox.

Fig. 3 Success in competition is the reward for hard training and good racing

For domestic competition it is necessary to have additional classes such as novice (never having won a qualifying race), and other categories based on age, experience and past successes. Thus there is fair competition and a ladder of success that the novice or youngster can climb as he or she develops in the sport. The ultimate to which talented and dedicated athletes can aim is to represent their country in a major international event – an experience that could well be the memory of a lifetime. For those who do not reach such heights, there is still an enormous amount of pleasure to be derived from striving (and sometimes succeeding) against others of similar standard.

In order to get the most out of your sport, you must be aware of the current standards, the way in which they are changing, and what factors determine performance. Then you can not only choose the most appropriate events but can also best seek ways in which to improve your chances of success – and that's what this book is all about.

IMPROVEMENT IN PERFORMANCE

Competitive standards continually rise both in domestic events and on the international stage. One reason for this is that there are far more athletes and coaches who are taking the necessary steps to success and ensuring that their equipment, training and technique is as good as it can be. There is also no doubt that there have been significant improvements in all three of those performance-determining factors in recent years.

FISA set minimum weight limits for the different classes of boat many years ago, and lightweight carbon fibre oars and sculls have also been around for a long while as well, but such equipment is now commonplace and not just restricted to the top crews. Blade shapes changed some time ago, but now we better understand how to use them. So, the best boats may not be any lighter but they are better constructed from modern synthetic materials and their shapes and ancillaries have continued to evolve.

The physical standards of the athletes have probably changed most and this is partly due to the general improvements in nutrition, health and physique in much of the world, but also as a result of improved recruiting and selection procedures. In particular it is apparent that the science of physiology has made great strides and consequently today's training methods have a much sounder scientific basis and are much more effective.

If we look at the results from the major international regattas over the last decade or so we can calculate the probable trend of reduction in average race times year on year. Of course the times actually fluctuate greatly, reflecting the great importance of wind and water conditions on the day. Nevertheless the figure seems to be reasonably reliable at a

Fig. 4 The physique of the best crews in the world may seem daunting, but much smaller people are also successful. These are the women's lightweight double scull medallists at the World Championships

little over 1 second per year (1.3 sec/yr, or 0.32%/yr) for men's crews and rather more for women and juniors (up to 0.5%/yr). Looked at another way this means that the men's gold medallists from one Olympiad would need to be about 5 seconds faster to retain their title at the next games. This perhaps puts a different perspective on the staggering achievements of Sir Steve Redgrave and Sir Matthew Pinsent in gaining five and four successive golds respectively. I suggest that most of their progress came from their own bodies and only a little from better equipment. In general the suggested change has been much the same for all boat classes but it does seem that smaller boats, and lightweights, are affected more by weather conditions and thus their times vary more.

PERFORMANCE-DETERMINING FACTORS

In the succeeding chapters of this book I hope to show how you can optimize your speed and success in racing, and I suggest that will depend on five major factors:

1. *Physical factors*   air and water resistance
                             ergonomics and biomechanics
                             oar and scull efficiency
                             all-up weight
2. *The athlete's physiology* strength, endurance and speed
                             response to the environment
                             nutrition
3. *Skill and technique*
4. *Psychology*
5. *Tactics*

In the remaining part of this chapter we can examine briefly the way in which these factors, either singly or in combination, limit performance, and then in later chapters see what we can do to help ourselves.

Physical factors

Air and water resistance

Aerodynamically, the conventional racing boat is a mess, with different pieces of equipment and athlete sticking out to interfere with airflow.

Air speeds are low in still air which suggests that this factor is not very important, say about 10% of total resistance to movement, but that is still significant. In head winds the effect is demonstrably a major factor and some attempts can be made to minimize it.

Water resistance is the major form of drag that retards the boat and this is because the boat must displace water in order to float, and it will disturb the water and pass energy to it as it passes through. With oar propulsion we cannot go fast enough to plane like a speed boat, nor can we sustain hydrofoil lift for long (believe me both have been tried). The main energy losses occur in the turbulent wake created by the friction of the boat's skin against the water, and in the waves made by the boat's shape and size as it pushes the water aside. It is up to us to choose the craft with the smoothest skin and best hull shape (and many modern boats appear to be approaching the optimum), and to look after it very carefully. It is also important that our technique does not generate unnecessary fluctuations in speed nor extra waves.

Ergonomics and biomechanics

The correct relationship between the athlete and the equipment is vital for effective power production and for skilled technical movements. There is little to be gained from a choice of theoretically ideal equipment if it is badly adjusted or unsuited to the individual athlete. Fortunately the modern boat is designed to make changes relatively easy, and the rules that govern such things are becoming more clearly established (see Chapter 5).

Oar and scull efficiency

The details of the way in which an oar propels a boat are not simple, although as long ago as 1925 Gilbert C. Bourne's classic *Textbook of Oarsmanship* contained a clear analysis. To the greatest extent the blade acts as the fulcrum of a (second order) lever by which the boat is levered past successive pieces of water, thus the less the blade slips the better. Using the blade as a spoon to hurl water sternwards in the hope that Newtonian reaction will move the boat forwards is demonstrably less effective. Blade shapes have changed in recent years and it does make some difference, as described in Chapter 5.

All-up weight

The total weight of boat, equipment and crew has two retarding effects. First of all, as Archimedes tells us, the heavier the load the more the water will be displaced – and this then means that the hull will create larger waves and more friction as it moves through the water. Secondly, the boat does not travel at uniform speed – it must be accelerated at the start and must then be accelerated again and again as it loses speed in the recovery part of each stroke cycle. The greater mass needs more energy to accelerate it. There is a common fallacy that the heavier boat will gain by its greater inertia so that less speed is lost between strokes, but this view is not supported by calculation.

For example a 10 kg saving on a 100 kg eight, with a 50 kg cox and 85 kg average crew, using conventional wooden oars at 4 kg each, gives a saving of 0.26% on time. Assuming a best race time of 5 min 30 sec, this 0.26% improvement represents a 0.86 sec advantage. Many races are won by less than that! Change to carbon oars at fewer than 3 kg each and you can gain another 0.8 sec. In his book *Four Men in a Boat* Tim Foster points out that when the GB coxless four lost in Lucerne before the Sydney Olympics they were 15 kg overweight; they lost that surplus and won gold by 0.38 seconds. How much more crucial was the weight that the four lost before Athens for a winning margin of 0.08 seconds?

The athlete's physiology

Strength, endurance and speed

Such is the magnitude of the resistance encountered by a boat at speed that considerable strength is required to overcome it and maintain the speed. However, strength alone is not enough for it is essential to be able to overcome the resistance quickly, and this means *power*, a rather different quality. Maximal strength is only one component because it must also be combined with endurance to enable you to maintain adequate power for the duration of a race. There is no doubt that the most successful rowers tend to fall within a well-defined and muscular body-build or somatotype (fig. 5), and yet there are many exceptions. It is also true that most athletes,

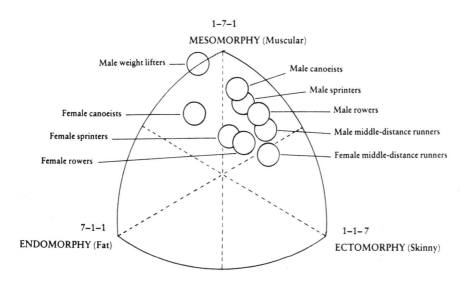

Fig. 5 Typical somatotypes (body-build) of Olympic competitors

forced to operate close to their maximal strength, will then suffer from a lack of endurance.

Three types of endurance can be identified and to some extent they have different physiological bases.

> *General endurance* – characteristic of low-level power outputs maintained for a long time.
>
> *Strength endurance* – the maintenance of a required high level of strength for a substantial period of time.
>
> *Speed endurance* – the ability to overcome a resistance quickly and repeatedly.

The 2,000-metre rowing course does require high levels of endurance, but this is of a type sometimes referred to as 'special endurance', i.e. specific to rowing that distance. This is largely *power endurance* – with strength and speed endurance as its principal components. The ability to row a long way slowly does not by itself win races.

Fortunately these desirable characteristics, whilst to some extent inherited, can also be much developed by appropriate training – and your effort will be rewarded. It is also important to realize that the response is specific to the type of training employed; what you get out of it depends on what you put into it. Chapters 6 and 7 explain the mix of training that is required.

Response to the environment

Whether indoors or out our bodies respond to environmental conditions in order to maintain the quite narrow range of internal states within which we function best. We have the adaptability to survive very adverse environments but we cannot perform well if our resources are diverted, or if we fail to adjust fully. Some of the problems and ways of minimizing them are described in Chapter 9.

Nutrition

In a sense we are what we eat, although most of what we eat is quickly used up, and the rest is highly modified before it is incorporated into our bodies. Without good nutrition we cannot grow to our full genetic potential and we cannot release energy from our food in the optimum way for training or competition. On the other hand there is no evidence that there is any magic dietary formula that will ensure higher performance – after all, the many champions are likely to all have different dietary preferences. However it is a very important matter and there are well-accepted dietary guidelines that you would be wise to observe. One international athlete once said that, like gamblers, we are always on the lookout for some special ingredient that will turn us into supermen, if not overnight, at least by next Saturday. Chapter 9 will tell you the guidelines to follow and help you to avoid wasting time and money on quack remedies.

Skill and technique

The technique of both rowing and sculling has the twin aims of enabling you to make the best use of your physique and physical capabilities, and to move the blade through the most effective pattern both in and out of the water. We should also be aiming to carry out the movements in a smooth and rhythmic way that minimizes energy loss.

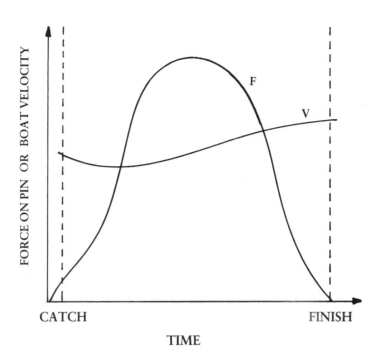

Fig. 6 Variations in force on the pin and in boat velocity during the stroke

It is characteristic of the action that large masses move in ways that adversely affect the smooth flow of the boat through the water, and that the variations in both power output and speed during the stroke reduce overall speed (fig. 6).

In the main stream of world class rowing today, it is apparent that eccentric styles have all but vanished, and there is general uniformity of technique. The best athletes show economy of movement and a lack of any exaggerated positions of either the legs or back; they are thus enabled to use their muscle groups over their most effective range. Bladework too, at its best, shows the simple attributes of a fast catch at full reach, a level drive through the water, and a fast, clean extraction – no frills or violent movements. Such deceptively simple skills are hard to acquire, hard to maintain in the stress of competition, and will require hours of patient attention to detail under all conditions and pressures. As previously mentioned good technique is also a function of good equipment properly adjusted and maintained.

Skeletal muscles contract and relax according to the instructions they receive from the nervous system. Rowing is notable for the very large number of muscle groups involved not only in propelling the boat but also in the essential movements of technique and in balancing the craft. To achieve this complexity a phenomenal amount of sensory information from the organs of touch, pressure, stretch, sight, and so on, must be processed by the central nervous system and used to direct the appropriate responses of the muscles. Thus skilled movements are the result of the precisely timed contraction and relaxation of a myriad disparate muscle fibres.

We can assume then that the successful competitor will possess highly developed sensory and motor nervous systems, which will show themselves as technical skill and very effective movement patterns. Nevertheless handicapped athletes can find that this rhythmic action in a supportive craft suits them very well and adaptive rowing is rightly growing in popularity. The maintenance of skill under race conditions or in hard training will be greatly affected by shortage of oxygen and by a number of waste products of metabolism. It follows then that the competitors whose physiology, training or tactics spares them most from such ill effects will be at a further advantage. It is equally true that time spent learning and establishing skills under pressure is doubly valuable, but that basic technical grounding is best carried out free from other stresses.

Coxing too is a physical skill requiring a great deal of practice in all conditions in order to acquire the necessary feel for the water and for the boat's behaviour. The good cox can follow the optimum course with the minimum disturbance to the boat's run and balance.

Psychology

Competitive rowing and its essential tough training are very demanding not only on the physical abilities of the athlete but also on a wide range of personality factors. A detailed study of these factors is beyond the scope of this book but they are touched upon later. It is clear that at the top level there is little to separate the physical attributes of the potential champions, and their equipment may well be identical, so the ultimate performance comes from those who combine those attributes with the most suitable mental approach. Developing the physical sides in itself demands dedicated and effective training over many years and requires exceptional determination and persistence. Without the right psychology the learning process will not be effective, and at the same time the mental strengths must be developed to cope with increasingly tough

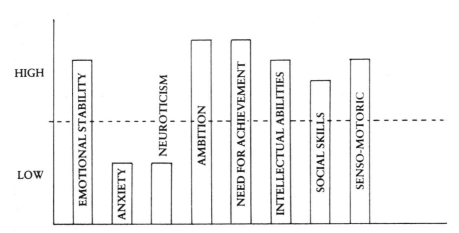

Fig. 7 Psychological characteristics of good competitors

training and competition. In the competition itself the best competitor is not just very tough-minded, but has the ability to retain control under extreme pressure so that technique and tactics are optimized (fig. 7).

Essentially the successful competitor is selfish. Loyalty to state, club or friends may be important at times, but in the end athletes want victory for themselves to meet their personal need for satisfaction, whatever its origin. And winning is not necessarily everything – knowing that you have done your absolute best in the most demanding circumstances can also be very rewarding. This is not to deny the importance of personal relationships, whether with coach, family, friends or other crew members. In the last case, perhaps we can claim that crew rowing must be the ultimate team sport, where so much must be sublimated by the individual for the common good.

The cox also has much to contribute to the responses and morale of the crew, both during racing and in the long preparation for it. The cox's role can be a vital one in maintaining concentration on the desired training or competitive goals and in giving essential feedback and encouragement to the crew. Particularly in the larger boats, the cox does much to aid communication and hence cohesion, and is the essential mouthpiece of the stroke, and often the coach too.

Race tactics

Race tactics have both physical and psychological effects. To win a race against good opposition means working close to your limits (or what you perceive to be your limits) and the wrong choice of tactics can mean that excessive fatigue comes too soon. It is characteristic of our sport that a very small increase in speed demands a disproportionate increase in power (roughly the cube!), and we must be sure that its benefits are really worthwhile. If you are confident in your race plan, however, and your tactical moves seem to be having their desired effect, then there will be a psychological boost for you and perhaps a blow for your opponent, which can be worth more than any loss of economy.

2 Sculling Technique

At its most basic, technique means simply the way in which you propel the boat through the water, but for competition purposes the requirement is for a technique that will use your physical capacity to the full in propelling the boat as quickly as possible. A good, efficient technique is essential for the best enjoyment of the sport, whether the aim is success in racing and knowing that you have made the most of your efforts, or just in the pleasure of mastery of your craft. In addition good technique will enable you to cope with adverse weather and water conditions. For both the beginner and the experienced competitor the development of these skills and their maintenance under pressure is extremely important. In their books both Tim Foster and Matthew Pinsent are clear that technical weaknesses lost them important races before their Olympic triumphs.

Most newcomers to the sport will start by learning to scull, and in many countries children under the age of 14 or 15 are only permitted to scull (not row) in open competition. Even those who did not start that way should learn to scull, for the single sculling boat is a wonderful aid to learning the skills of boat moving and balance. There are very good arguments to support the idea that young beginners should scull rather than row. On the technical side these include the fact that youngsters before puberty have an exceptional ability to learn quickly how to balance the craft, and that because the action is symmetrical the young athlete does not learn an early preference for one side of the boat. It has been claimed that the asymmetry of rowing can be harmful to the developing spine, but there is little real evidence for this, or that rowers have more back problems than scullers. I do not believe that doing a bit of rowing as well would harm young athletes. Furthermore, most top-class rowers do a lot of training in single sculls as an aid to fitness, technique and psychology.

There are practical difficulties if beginners are to start in single sculls, for it is essential to have good safe water and weather conditions, suitable equipment and close supervision. I am not convinced that things like playboats are the answer, even though they may be fun, because they are too unlike a real sculling boat and too insensitive to give good feedback. In good conditions the young beginner will quickly learn to handle a narrow, but short and light boat, but in less favourable circumstances or with older novices, the coxed quad is likely to be the best choice.

The single sculling boat is both the greatest challenge and the most rewarding type of boat. Only your unaided efforts will move it, and in order to move it well you will need real skill and also understanding of the nature of wind and water (the qualities that are prized as 'watermanship'). As a learning vehicle it is often ideal, for it is so responsive that the sculler learns from it how to get the best results. The beginner is free from the problems caused by clumsy crewmates and from the need to keep in time with others, whilst even the most experienced athlete can always learn more from its subtleties. The double scull and the quad are also very rewarding because they are so fast – faster than the same number of athletes rowing – but challenging because twice as many blades need to be co-ordinated.

Sculling technique differs from rowing in a number of ways, primarily because the two arms describe two opposite arcs, and also because the handles overlap so the hands must cross at some point in the stroke. The movement of the hands is not quite symmetrical, nor is that of the blades; because the hands cross, they must pass either one in front of the other, or one above the other. Particularly in the single scull the balance problems are different to those in rowing; the boat is narrower, the sculls are shorter than oars and each athlete has two of them. Thus the control of hand heights and movements becomes especially crucial.

GETTING INTO THE BOAT

Warming up and loosening on land should precede every outing and once you are out on the water you should follow a physical and technical warm-up. You should start with simple relaxed exercises and work up to more demanding skills and speeds. The particular technical aims of the outing should be rehearsed at this time while you are still fresh, but already warm and flexible.

Before you put the boat into the water make sure that both gates are undone, and that the sculls are within easy reach. Put both sculls into their gates (**R**ed on the **R**ight hand) and do up the gate that is nearer to you – don't crawl over the boat to try and do up the far gate. Facing the stern, grasp both handles firmly together in the hand nearer the boat. Making sure that the buttons are firmly against the swivels, push the seat out of the way towards the bows and step carefully onto the centre section of the boat (most have a non-slip pad here) with the foot that is nearer the boat. Expert scullers will now push off with the other foot before they sit down. Gently lower yourself onto the seat, if necessary steadying yourself with your free hand at the point where the rigger meets the shoulder. Swing the free foot into place in its shoe, followed by the other. You will now have to change hands or tuck the handles under your armpits while you do up the other gate or make adjustments – but don't let go!

Assuming that your boat and sculls are suitably rigged for you, and if not refer to Chapter 5 for the correct measurements, you need to make sure that the stretcher is in the correct place. If you sit at the finish position, legs straight, hands on the handles about 10–15 cm apart, upper body leaning back about 20–30 degrees, then the handles should be just in front of your chest and you could touch your chest with your thumbs. Move the stretcher until you can achieve this position and then check that you will not contact frontstops as you slide forwards. Some coaches suggest that light contact of the seat with backstops is desirable, but if the slides are long and your legs are not then you may never reach either end, and it doesn't matter.

HOLDING THE SCULLS

The scull handle is small enough to fit nicely into the curved fingers and should be held there and never in the palm. The thumb is kept loosely on the end of the handle, not underneath. In all parts of the stroke the wrists should be kept as flat as possible with squaring and feathering achieved by rolling the handles in the fingers. During the recovery the handles can be guided by a loose hold out in the fingers. To square the blades roll the fingers round the handles, perhaps aided by pressure from the thumbs, so that the handles then fit into the roots of the fingers and the wrists are not raised. The wrists should remain flat or slightly arched throughout the catch and drive, and then it is possible for the lower (right) hand to fit snugly under the hollow of the upper (left) wrist when the hands cross

Fig. 8 The hands overlap in the middle of the stroke with the left hand uppermost. The thumbs are on the ends of the handles, which are held in the base of the fingers

– this enables the hands to be kept close together without colliding. Ideally the upper, left, hand is always a little further from the body so that during the recovery the hands may again cross without interference. From your point of view the left hand leads away from the finish above the right and during the pull the right hand is nearer to you and leading the way. Feathering should be done with the minimum of wrist work by opening the hands, and pushing with the thumbs if necessary, so that the handles are rolled out into the relaxed fingers again. It is a good idea to keep the fingernails short, especially on the left hand.

THE CYCLE OF THE STROKE

The recovery

From the finish the hands should lead away, left above right and in front, smoothly and without pause at a controlled speed related to the speed through the water. The back should be held firm and the head up

Fig. 9 a–h Sculling technique sequence

a *Approaching the catch* The body is compressed against the thighs, shins vertical. Arms fully extended but not stiff. The blades are rolled onto the square position with the thumb and fingers, wrists flat.

b *The catch* The blades are covered quickly with straight arms. The leg drive and opening of the body angle occurs simultaneously.

c *The Drive* The strong leg drive is transmitted through a firm back and straight arms. Note the overlap of the hands. The blades are fully covered.

d *Approaching the finish* As the leg drive comes to an end the arms bend and draw. Note the good position of the hands as they overlap and the excellent depth of the blades.

e *The finish* The hands move down to lift the blades from the water and the blades are feathered by rolling the handle into the fingers together with a slight drop of the wrists.

f *The recovery* The hands move away first while the knees are held down. As the hands cross the left hand will be on top and could be a little in advance of the right.

g *The recovery* The hands are now ahead of the knees, which are now rising. The body is swinging over. Note the overlap of the hands and the relaxed arms.

h *The recovery* The body is swung over and the arms nearly fully extended as the legs flex. Note the good balance and the height of the blades above the water.

but the legs remain straight at this stage. As the arms extend the upper body swings over and although the hamstrings can relax the knees should not rise appreciably until the hands are clear. The wrists can by now have regained their flat position and there should be a loose hold of the handles such that the forearm muscles can relax. As the knees begin to bend they should be close together.

On the way forward the fully feathered blades should be safely clear of the water but not too high, on smooth water 10–15 cm would be enough. On modern high rigs the looms will slope down from the hands towards the water but there will still be plenty of room to drop the hands if the blades need to clear waves. The arms will now be well extended but not completely straight and certainly not stiff. Most of the body swing has already been accomplished as the legs flex and the seat approaches front stops. All movements must be smooth, unhurried and steady with the objective of not disturbing the flow of the boat by any harsh acceleration or braking. Keep the knees together and the hands at more or less the same height.

Fully forward

Approaching this position the sculler will be fully extending the arms and shoulders, but without tension, and will square the sculls as described earlier, keeping the lower edge of the blade close to the water. The hands will move a long way apart and the sensation should be that you are pushing out almost sideways before you take the catch. The fingers should be as relaxed as possible so that you feel that you are about to drop the sculls into the water at full reach, where the sculls will be at about 30 degrees to the boat. The seat will slow gradually as it approaches frontstops and it is important that the upper body does not dive over the knees – keeping the head up so that you are looking well astern helps to maintain the best body position for the catch. The chest will come into light contact with the thighs as it leans forward about 10-30 degrees and it is most comfortable if the knees separate a little. At this point the heels will be lifted from the stretcher, and the shins will be vertical or nearly so depending on your leg length.

Fig. 10 The hands separate widely for the catch. The acute angle of the sculls to the boat is crucial for the most effective catch

The catch

A very rapid lift of the hands is required to cover the blades quickly and this comes from a movement of the arms from the shoulders, not by bending the arms. At the same time the legs must start driving and the upper body start its swing. The ideal is for power to be applied as the blade enters the water so that very little of the effective length of the stroke is lost. Performed correctly there will be only a small splash of water upwards from the blade. Too slow an entry and water will hit the back of the blade, act as a brake and be thrown towards the bows. Too shallow an entry, or rowing in the blade with power applied too soon, will be shown by water being thrown sternwards off the face of the blade.

Gripping the handles before the catch tends to make the movement slower and clumsier and you should try to be relaxed. Because of the acute angle of the sculls to the boat at the catch, a fast beginning in a sculling boat gives the feeling that the hands move towards each other very quickly, as indeed they should do. Of course the two blades should take the water exactly together and this requires that not only is the boat well balanced but that you are too; you are 'on your feet', firmly located on the stretcher and confident in the location of both blades in relation to the water – the catch must not be tentative.

The drive

Particularly in the single scull the drive is somewhat more sustained and progressive than in rowing; smooth acceleration is the keynote. The drive is initially through straight arms and with a firm back to link the leg action to the handles. The two blades must be driven through just nicely covered. It is now commonly accepted that the rigging height should be more than was generally recommended before and for most people heights of 16–18 cm or more are usual. Such heights give an efficient angle of pull and at the same time help prevent the blades going too deep, and are particularly suited to the 'big blades' and the

Fig. 11 The height of the gates leaves plenty of room for the feathered blades to clear the water on the recovery. It is usual to set the left gate higher than the right to allow for the overlap

Fig. 12 This sculler is bending his arms much too early

technique that goes with them. As the sculls approach the right angle the handles will overlap. As described earlier the right hand will be nearer the body, and the left hand on top but not by too much. To allow for this it is common to have the left rigger set about 1 cm higher.

In sculling the arms will bend earlier than in rowing, but there should be no deliberate attempt to use the arms early or there may be a slower initial drive and the arms will fatigue sooner. Video analysis shows that from the catch in sculling the upper body moves faster than the seat as compared with rowing; that is, the body angle opened faster in relation to the leg drive. It is common to see these differences when the same athlete is sculling or rowing. The reasons may be that firstly the sculler reaches to a more acute angle, and secondly that the sculler is provided with a greater blade area giving less slip.

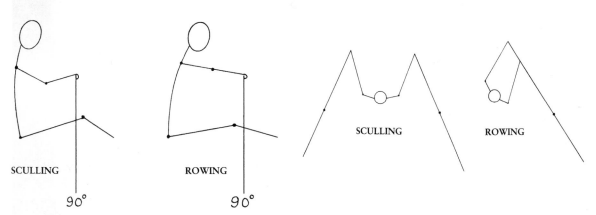

Fig. 13 Video analysis shows that the body position in sculling does differ from that in rowing

Fig. 14 The angle of the arms to the handle is different in sculling as compared with rowing

The draw

From the right angle position to the finish the sculls will sweep through a further 30 degrees or so. The force will be diminishing in this phase but the aim will be to continue the steady acceleration of the system. The vigorous opening of the body angle in the first part of the stroke should ensure that some leg drive remains to be used and this is added to with a vigorous (but not violent) final use of the arms and shoulders. With high riggers it is necessary to allow the elbows to point out to the sides some-what to avoid a cramped position and over flexed wrists. There is a danger of washing out and the blade must be kept covered. Fortunately the blade now has a mound of water in front of it which helps to keep it covered, and also the slide slopes upwards from front to back stops, thus reducing the effective rigger height towards the finish. On the other hand the blades should not be excessively deep or speed will be lost and a messy finish will result. Strong core muscles and good posture are essential.

The finish

Pressure should be maintained on the blades until the last possible moment so that a mound of water remains on the face of the blade and a cavity behind it. The forearms and hands do not have to be brought down very much to lift the blades quickly and cleanly from the water, and as they do so the hands unroll and the blades start to feather (helped by a small and brief deflection of the wrist if necessary). At this

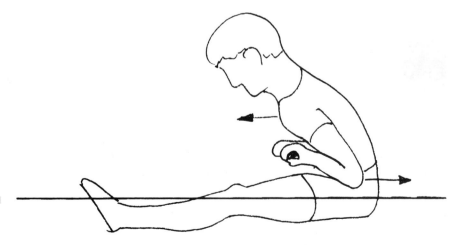

Fig. 15 Bucking the finish means that power is reduced as the sculler collapses forward rather than maintaining the draw to the end of the stroke

point the hands will be about 10–15 cm apart and will probably separate a little more as the blades continue sternwards a fraction – but the
hands stay in front of the body and should not contact it before moving
away into the recovery. The anatomy of scullers differs and so do their
styles but it is probable that an angle of layback of no more than 20–30
degrees will be best. Many scullers slump at the finish but it is better for
both breathing and technique to sit up in a more commanding position.

BALANCE

A bicycle is much more unstable than even the finest sculling boat, yet
most people learn to balance the machine very quickly. Once learnt the
skill becomes automatic and unconscious and indeed it is only when we
no longer have to think about it that we do it well. So it is with sculling.
The skill of good balance is vital to enjoyment and good performance,
but knowing the theory is no substitute for practice in the boat until the
necessary actions become second nature. The overriding principle is

Fig. 16 For good balance the
two sculls should finish together
with the left hand a little higher
than the right (assuming the left
gate is set higher)

never to practise sloppy technique and be determined to make the boat run smoothly, level, and with the blades clear of the water throughout the recovery.

If you swing straight, keep your head steady, sit evenly on the seat with both feet well planted on the stretcher, and take catches and finishes simultaneously with both sculls, then the boat should run level. In practice of course things are not that easy! There are some common faults that can lead to balance problems and the sculler or coach should check for these first.

Uneven finishes

Fig. 17 In rough water good balance skills and blades that are higher off the water will be needed

Because of the way in which the hands cross, it is often the case that the hands finish at different heights or at different times, and inevitably the boat will tip at the finish and will not be stable for the recovery. Again because of the asymmetry of the hand action, it is not uncommon for one

scull to be cleared from the water and feathered before the other, and this is sufficient to upset the boat. The correct hold of the handles and feathering action will help to prevent these problems, and this can be practised with single-stroke exercises. Even worse are the sorts of lazy finishes that allow the water to catch up with the blades or drags them out across the surface. I believe that crisp, clean and well-synchronized finishes are the most important factor in establishing good balance.

Hand heights

A sculling boat is greatly affected by the relative positions of the two sculls during the recovery. I have already advocated the technique where the left hand leads the recovery so that the hands and boat can both be level. With one hand in front of the other it is then possible to make fine adjustments to the boat's equilibrium by raising or lowering the hands independently. As the full reach position is approached the sculls are closing in towards the sides of the boat and their stabilizing effect is lessened – so balance becomes more critical and even pressure on the feet and with the hands is even more important. As the blades are squared and their height above the water adjusted any discrepancies between the two sides can lead to a loss of balance and uneven catches.

Uneven pressure on the swivels

Sometimes a dragged finish, or one hand being pulled back too far, will actually cause the button to be pulled away from the swivel. This is easy to spot, but less overt differences in outward pressure can also mar the recovery. In fact pushing out more on one side than the other is one way in which you can legitimately correct a wobble or even a persistent crosswind, but this is best done with just the hands and arms rather than a crude lean with the whole upper body.

Uneven pressure on the feet

Sculling with one hand in front of the other can cause a rotation of the shoulders and also perhaps a slight turn of the pelvis so that the legs do not quite move together. Many scullers do in fact partly balance the

Fig. 18 The legs should go down together or efficiency and balance will be lost

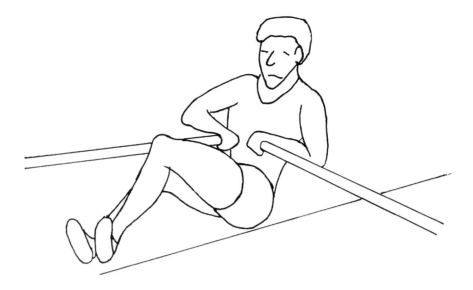

boat by sideways movement of the knees in the later stages of the recovery, and by adjusting the pressure of the feet on the stretcher. This is a valid technique but the snag is that the ideal catch and drive comes from evenly placed, indeed firmly planted, feet on the stretcher – so it should not be overdone.

CREW SCULLING

As was mentioned at the beginning of the chapter, the double scull and quad are faster than their rowing equivalents, so one of the requirements for success in these boats is the ability to maintain good sculling technique whilst moving very quickly. Synchronization of all the actions is also vital and it is often helpful if the crew sculler has also had experience of crew rowing. The best crew scullers will also be good single scullers and the more sensitive single is a better vehicle for learning balance and watermanship. On the other hand single scullers often develop idiosyncrasies and some find it hard to adapt to the different discipline of the crew boat. Experience in the larger boats is valuable and the quicker action can in turn help the single sculler to be lively. Because the quad in particular is relatively stable, it is an easy but rewarding boat for beginners and youngsters, and it also makes coaching for a uniform technique much easier (and possibly safer) than four singles.

Fig. 19 A young composite quad battles to a close finish at Henley

Because there are so many technical points to watch for in a more advanced double, quad or octuple, I would suggest that frequent use of the video is essential. I do not believe that the coach's unaided eye can cope with so many things happening at once, and the athletes need all the feedback they can get if they are to integrate perfectly.

EXERCISES FOR BEGINNERS AND IMPROVERS

In order to make progress the sculler must develop confidence in controlling and balancing the boat before trying to move it quickly, and exercises and games such as the following will help to achieve this.

1   Familiarity and confidence in the stationary boat. Keep the scull blades flat on the water and lean the body from side to side whilst holding the handles together in front of the body – the boat does not tip over. Raise and lower alternate hands – note which way the boat tips and how easy it is to recover. For how long can you balance the boat with both sculls clear of the water? The extension of this is to balance the boat with the handles jammed on the opposite saxboards, hands free – perhaps even standing on the seat?

2   Lean the boat slightly to one side so that it is supported by one

scull. Sitting at backstops, scull the boat round in a circle with the other hand and practise squaring and feathering at the same time; now change hands and go round the other way. Alternate backing down and paddling on opposite sides to spin the boat – initially one stroke at a time with the boat supported on the other scull, and then both at the same time.

3 Scull with arms only and the legs straight, initially with square blades. Continue by introducing fractions of the slide, keeping a particular emphasis on clean finishes. How far can you scull with square blades without them touching the water?

4 Practise taking corners, without changing rhythm nor pulling with only one hand, by reaching a little further with the scull on the outside of the bend. Note that extra reach will move the bows round the way you want to go much more effectively than longer or harder finishes. Try to keep your head up and look well astern to judge whether you are steering the best course, but don't forget to look round frequently to check you are safe. Slalom races between buoys are good fun, as is 'leapfrogging' with a partner where you overtake and then pull in while your partner goes past.

5 Loosen the fingers during the recovery until you can keep the fingers flat on top of the handles, just guiding them rather than holding them.

There are a number of other exercises in the next chapter, which can be adapted for single or crew sculling, and which will help to improve both individual technique and crew co-ordination and cohesion.

Once these elementary skills are mastered, the need is to refine the full technique still further and to make the skills automatic so that full power can be applied smoothly and rhythmically and the boat runs without check. 'Mileage makes champions' perhaps, but not if the prospective champions do not have a clear image of what they are attempting to achieve and how to achieve it, and not unless they are given lots of reinforcement and feedback. In single sculling in particular it is all too easy to develop idiosyncrasies and trick movements, often without realizing it. So every outing must have a technical objective and the success of the effort must be felt and seen, while at the same time the other skills must not be allowed to deteriorate.

In the next chapter, on rowing technique, there is more discussion of the ergonomics and biomechanics, and knowledge of the principles will make you a better sculler and rower.

Fig. 20 Dutch and Australian quads show excellent technique at Henley

3 Rowing Technique

Good rowing and sculling technique is essentially simple – it is the faults that cause the complications – but it is highly skilled and it can take a long time to refine and perfect, especially if bad habits have been learnt and are allowed to intrude. It can be very difficult to 'unlearn' incorrect movements. There is also often confusion with 'style', which we can define as the distinctive body movements and varieties of bladework that are used. The fact that different styles are demonstrably equally effective suggests that the differences are not important, but it is also apparent that all successful styles have an essential technique in common, and it on this that you must concentrate.

For convenience of analysis we may divide the technique of rowing into four main areas:

1 The path of the blade into, through and out of the water – 'bladework'.
2 The co-ordinated muscular actions that produce the bladework and harness the athlete's power to move the boat.
3 Balance.
4 The rhythm of the stroke.

In the following pages I describe what constitutes good technique in these respects, and suggest ways in which you can master it, and then go on to explain some of the reasoning behind it. Of course, in reality the stroke is a fluid and continuous integration of all four factors, and they are mutually dependent.

POSITION IN THE BOAT

Before a stroke is taken it is essential to ensure that you are correctly seated, that stretchers and riggers and oars are suitably adjusted, and that the handle is being held correctly. You are in contact with the boat through three points: the seat, your feet on the stretcher, and your hands on the handle. It is through these that both boat and blade must be controlled. The boatbuilder is responsible for providing much of the relationship between riggers, seat and stretcher, as is described in Chapter 5, but boats have considerable adjustment available so that they can be made suitable for most ranges of rowing styles and sizes of athlete. More will be said later in this chapter about the importance of the adjustments in determining the effectiveness of particular aspects of technique, and the whole aspect of rigging is explored in detail in Chapter 5.

For the moment let us assume that all is well. Both buttocks are evenly placed on the hollows of the seat, and the stretcher is placed so that you can use the entire slide without hitting the stops (though some may prefer that the seat wheels be just in contact with the backstops when the legs are fully extended). For most rowers the aft edge of the seat should then be about 46–48 cm from a line across the boat through the pin. When sitting at that position the end of the handle should come to just beyond the side of the ribcage when you are sitting tall and leaning back and slightly towards the rigger. This is the position that we should aim for at the end of every stroke and it should be possible to hold the end of the handle with the appropriate hand to the side of the ribs, not in front. From that position it should be possible to extract the blade fully and square before you contact the thighs. With the arms straight and the blade just covered, the hands should be about 10 degrees below the shoulders.

If these basic positions cannot be achieved then the rigging is not right and should be corrected before you go any further.

HOLDING THE HANDLE

The correct hold on the handle is vital for skill and power, and even with very experienced athletes technical problems and faults can often be traced to this point. The hand furthest from the rigger (the outside hand) should be hooked round the last few centimetres of the handle so that the little finger can be tucked over the end. This stops it slipping down the handle and makes it easier to maintain a light outward pressure against the swivel. The handle should rest in the base of the fingers with the wrist flat or slightly arched and the

Fig. 21 Redgrave and Pinsent show a relaxed hold of the handles whilst racing at Henley

Fig. 22 The hands should be at least two hand-widths apart. Cracknell and Pinsent favoured traditional wooden handles

thumb hanging down below the handle. This hand should never grip but allow the handle to rotate. Tension and gripping with the outside hand causes clumsy movements, problems with feathering and possibly blisters and wrist pain. Think of guiding the oar through its desired path with the fingers of this outside hand, and use it merely as a hook when pulling through the stroke – do not grip.

The inside hand should not grip the handle tightly either. This is the hand for feathering and squaring the blade, and all that is required is that the handle is rolled out into the fingers to feather the blade, and then gathered back into the roots of the fingers with the wrist arching slightly in order to square it again. As with the other hand a tight grip will lead to clumsy actions and difficulty in feathering, and because the wrist will have to be used excessively, fatigue and cramp may soon set in with the possible danger of tenosynovitis in the longer term. Even in rough water it is rarely necessary to grip the handle, as the swivel face will hold it at the correct angle for you. If the blade does hit a wave it is better that loose hands and arms allow it to deflect rather than upset the whole boat. Most people find it best to have the hands about two hand-widths apart – a narrower placing constricts the finish action, whilst a wider one reduces power and control.

Fig. 23 In rough water it is important to remain relaxed so that if the blade does hit a wave the whole boat is not upset

Fig. 24 Adjustable plastic handles have their advantages but some forms can be slippery when wet and others may cause blisters

BLADEWORK

The essence of good bladework is that the blade must be covered as quickly as possible, and power applied as it bites the water so that minimum distance is lost. Then the blade is driven horizontally through the water with the blade just covered all the way, before a quick and clean release that neither allows water to strike the back of the blade nor throws water sternwards. During the recovery the blade should be just far enough from the surface to clear any waves, and to allow the blade to be squared without having neither to be raised nor risk catching the surface. As the blade squares it should be brought close to the surface in order to minimize the vertical movement required for the catch.

Figure 25 shows the ideal path of the blade, and the sequence of photographs in fig. 26 illustrates the movements of hands and body required to produce this bladework. It must be emphasized that the

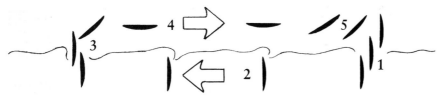

Fig. 25 Bladework

1 The blade is driven steeply and quickly into the water.
2 Blade just covered, constant depth.
3 Blade is extracted square, not feathered until clear of the water.
4 Blade kept clear of the water on the recovery.
5 Blade is brought down to the water as it is squared.

object is to anchor the blade in the water as quickly as possible at the beginning of the stroke, and that full power must be applied at that instant in order to lever the boat past that fixed point. To achieve this requires excellent co-ordination of the power muscles of the legs and trunk, together with the rapid lift of the hands that guides the blade into the water. Any excess vertical movements represent wasted energy – energy that is not moving the boat forwards but upwards or downwards. A blade that is not quickly covered at the catch, or is too shallow later in the stroke (washing out), may make an impressive-looking puddle, but it is heating the water rather than moving the boat. If the blade is too deep, then part of the loom will also be underwater and will be dragged backwards by the boat, acting as a brake.

STYLES

In the late 1960s Karl Adam and his great Ratzeburg crews revolutionized thinking about rowing technique and equipment. The essence of his method was that since the leg muscles are the most powerful and the most trainable, then most emphasis should be put upon leg action, and less done with the upper body. In order to achieve greater leg movement the slides needed to be lengthened, and the relationship between seat and feet altered. Inevitably when the athletes moved into the compressed forward position their heels rose from the stretcher, and so the fixed flexible rowing shoe was developed. The West German Ratzeburg eight won the 1968 Olympics and the new ideas became widely copied, but East Germany (the DDR as it then was) soon came to dominate world rowing with a different style. The DDR crews used shorter slides and consequently less leg compression and more body swing (fig. 28).

Fig. 26 Rowing technique sequence

a *Approaching the catch* The arms are extended and the shoulders rotating as the final part of the slide is used. The body swing has already been completed. The blade is squared close to the water using the inside hand.

b *Ready for the catch* Head up, looking astern. Full body compression with shins vertical. Blade close to the water.

c *The catch* The hands lift to just cover the blade and the slight back-splash shows that the entry was quick without 'rowing it in'. The leg drive and simultaneous opening of the body angle has already begun.

d *The drive* Full power is applied through a firm back and straight arms. Note the excellent depth of the blade.

e *Approaching the finish* The arms and shoulders complete the draw as the leg drive comes to an end. Here slightly raised wrists are being used to keep the blade covered.

f *The finish* The hands move down to lift the blade square from the water. The inside hand will then feather the blade. Note that the athlete is sitting tall with his head up.

g *The recovery* The hands move away, wrists flat and fingers loose, followed by the upper body. The back is straight, i.e. the swing is from the hips not by bending the back. A slight bend in the knees eases tension in the hamstrings.

h *The recovery* The knees rise when the hands have gone past and the body swing continues. The arms are straight but without tension.

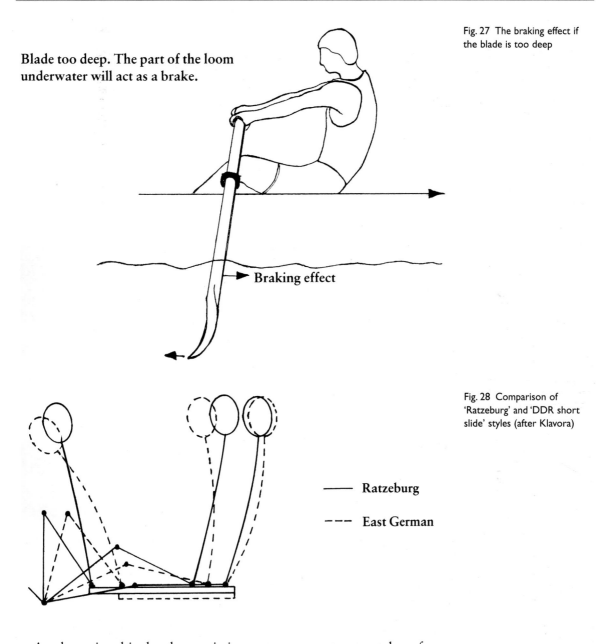

Blade too deep. The part of the loom underwater will act as a brake.

Fig. 27 The braking effect if the blade is too deep

Braking effect

Fig. 28 Comparison of 'Ratzeburg' and 'DDR short slide' styles (after Klavora)

—— Ratzeburg

--- East German

At championship level now it is rare to see extreme styles of any sort. Coaches are much more aware of biomechanics, and the technique now common avoids acute joint angles as inefficient and at the same time attempts to maximize power production from both legs and upper body. It is now accepted that the two extreme styles both had disadvantages and that a compromise between the two has most to commend it. It should be remembered that every athlete is an individual and variations from whatever is regarded as ideal are not only probable, but may even be desirable to make the most of individual qualities. We should not attempt to copy slavishly, but to observe, learn and apply the lessons to our own circumstances.

BALANCE

It is impossible to row well unless the boat is stable, but it is equally difficult to balance a boat unless it is being rowed well! A rolling boat will also create more resistance and require appreciably more energy to propel it than one which is running level. As a starting point then, it is essential for you to appreciate that good balance is important and that every crew member must strive not to upset the boat. Earlier it was stated that the boat is controlled through three contact points – the seat, the feet and the hands – but there is always the special problem that rowing is a crew sport and therefore all crew members must work together to balance the boat.

The rowing action is asymmetrical and therefore opposing crew members must act to cancel out the inherent imbalance. In particular

Fig. 29 Leaning away from the rigger can cause a weak and messy finish

we have seen that each rower should lean towards their own rigger, but it is very tempting to swing the body sideways in an effort to correct a loss of balance. Such movements are very undesirable, as they are too crude and merely cause further balance and other technical problems. Concentrate instead on sitting still and maintaining the outward pressure on your rigger; variations in that pressure can then be used to steady the boat. Similarly, every action of the stroke must be synchronized with the other crew member(s), but most particularly at the catches and finishes so that the blades enter and leave the water together.

If the crew is well together then the balance problems will be minimized and fine adjustments with the feet and hands are all that are required. Generally it is best if an even pressure can be maintained with both feet on the stretcher, but it can sometimes be helpful during the recovery part of the stroke to push down more with the foot on the side that is tending to rise. Although the oar only weighs a few kilos it is so long that it makes a very effective 'balancing pole', and small vertical movements of the hands can have a critical effect on balance. One of the primary tasks of the beginner is to learn the importance of blade control for this purpose. Pushing the hands down (and raising the blade) tends to make the boat roll towards your side and vice versa, but even the most experienced rowers find it all too tempting to push their hands down when the boat rolls their way – even though this makes the situation worse.

RHYTHM

One of the characteristics of the best athletes in any sport is that they seem to make it look easy – they seem to have a natural flowing rhythm that gives them time and enables them to expend their energy in the most efficient way. Nowhere is this more true than in rowing and sculling, where not only must the athlete's movements be as labour-saving as possible but also the smooth run of the boat must not be disturbed.

A fundamental requirement is that all movements are smooth, economical and unhurried, and fit together to form a continuous cycle of strokes. Within the cycle the part through the water is explosively powerful, but such speed can be accomplished without violence. The boat must accelerate through each stroke from catch to finish and it is important for you to strive for this feeling of a powerful (yet smooth) surge through the water and incorporate it in your mental image of the stroke. The hands maintain the terminal speed of the handle as they draw it to the finish and guide it round and away from the body. The aim is for a constant speed of the hands in a semicircular path as the blade is released from the water and begins the recovery. It is important to think of maintaining the momentum from one stroke to carry you forward into the next. The age old coaching cry of 'hands, body, slide' is still valid, partly for the practical reason that the hands must be clear of the knees before the knees rise, and partly because that sequence really is the best way to finish the stroke and start the recovery. Holding the legs down for a moment and the back firm gives the most stable basis for the action of the hands and arms as they complete the stroke and move the handle around the turn. Allowing the shoulders to move forwards too soon prevents the muscles in that area from maintaining their force and a weak finish will result (fig. 15). If the shoulders initiate the recovery rather than the arms, then the action will be slowed and the blade is likely to drag on the water at the finish.

Although the arms should be partly extended before the body starts to move, they should not be stiff – indeed it is very important that all parts of the body should be as relaxed as possible during the recovery. It is desirable that most of the body-swing is achieved before the seat moves away for three reasons. Firstly, it helps to transfer pressure on to the feet and thus stabilize the boat, secondly it avoids later changes in the height of the shoulders which are the common cause of poor bladework in the approach to the catch, and thirdly the delayed sliding helps to minimize the effect of the changing centre of gravity of the crew on the boat speed (see fig. 30).

All that is left now is to slide forward at a steady speed and use the hands, arms and shoulders to prepare for the catch. As has already been stated, any stiffness or rigidity is to be avoided but it is helpful to use the core trunk muscles to maintain a good upright posture, and keeping the head up will help this as well. A flatter back will be stronger when the catch is taken, and sitting tall helps to maintain the arms and shoulders in the best position for the catch (fig. 31). As you compress the legs and reach out for the catch, muscles and tendons are stretched and this effect can give extra power. On the other hand compressing too fast (rushing) can create problems with timing and balance and tends to bury the stern. Remember that you are trying to achieve a smooth, continuous and flowing stroke, so a controlled but

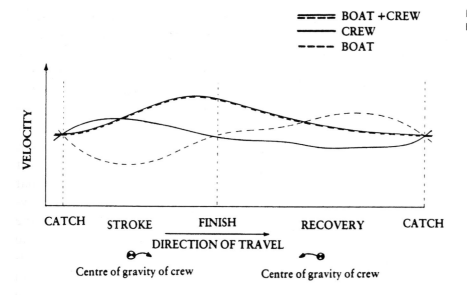

Fig. 30 Velocity changes of boat, crew, and both combined

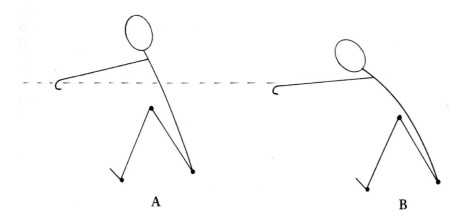

Fig. 31 Sitting up at the catch gives a better position and helps avoid dropping the hands and skying the blade

unchecked approach and a swift reversal at the catch are what you want. As you reach out for the catch the outside hand, arm and shoulder must reach further so the shoulders rotate towards the rigger – stiffness or excessive curvature in the spine hinders this swing, so sit up and stay relaxed. Most rowers find that a little flexion of the inside elbow also helps.

To sum up, the blade is driven quickly through the water, accelerating from catch to finish, and the hands maintain this final speed round the turn and away before the seat moves steadily down the slide. The recovery is therefore slower than the drive through the water, and a good rower will be able to retain this controlled and relaxed recovery even at very high speed.

It is easy to forget that the crew is much more massive than the boat itself (e.g. seven times more for a typical heavyweight eight) and consequently the movements of the crew up and down the boat have a large effect, by Newton's Law, on the speed of the boat. Fig. 30 shows the velocity variations that can be expected for boat and crew separately, and for the system as a whole. If you don't believe this just watch crews going for the line in a tight finish; who gets there first can depend on which part of their final stroke they are in.

Such variations in speed are inevitable, given the nature of the rowing cycle, but they do represent inefficiency because of the extra drag penalty of speeds greater than the average. It can be estimated that the total drag is increased about 3–4% as a result of this, but with sliding rigger systems now illegal it is difficult to see how any substantial improvements could be made. However, it does emphasize how important it is that the technique embodies a smooth rhythm without hurried movements by the crew.

LEARNING GOOD TECHNIQUE

Attitude is all-important, for it is essential to believe that technique is very important and can always be improved. With prolonged training the body adapts and movement patterns become automatic, and at the same time much easier and smoother. Unfortunately incorrect actions are as easy to learn as correct ones – remember that practice makes permanent, not perfect! The attitude to adopt must be that every stroke taken is an opportunity to improve technique, and this is a goal to strive for whatever the circumstances and however great the pressure. To do this unfailingly takes a lot of patience and much determination, but the dividends are great. It should not be forgotten that the novice and youngster simply cannot row in a mature way – the necessary muscle development, strength and co-ordination aren't there yet – but that doesn't mean that they should not be trying to get it right. With young rowers and scullers there is the added problem that growth will greatly affect their body proportions and co-ordination, and it is thus inevitable that their rowing technique must change.

There is no doubt that children learn motor skills much faster than older adolescents, who in turn learn faster than adults. Before puberty, children can learn skills such as balance very quickly, and it would be ideal to introduce children to the sport at that age. One of the problems is in providing suitable equipment, for many youngsters will be too small and weak to handle even cut-down adult boats and blades. The other problem is finding somewhere pleasant and safe to practise under the eye of a competent coach. The best teacher is the boat itself, but if the learners are to discover for themselves what they can do they must have a responsive craft. The ideal vehicles are single sculls and coxless pairs, and every ambitious rower should aim to become proficient in both, and be able to row on both sides. For practical reasons including safety, it may be better to start in larger and more stable craft and then go on to more challenging types.

At any stage of the learning process you must have a clear mental image of what is required. It is also a useful trick to rehearse mentally what you are going to do and how it will feel before you attempt the action. A verbal description is rarely enough and there is no substitute for actual experience – preferably on the water although tanks and ergometers can be good substitutes. Similarly, most of us do not respond adequately to simply being told that what we are doing is correct or not correct, and it is most valuable to see what was happening on video. Video analysis of the technique of model athletes is also extremely useful, and can often be more instructive than watching the real thing.

The whole stroke cannot be learnt at once, nor can we improve the whole stroke all at the same time. It is necessary to concentrate on each aspect, and not try to do too much in any one training session. We must never forget, however, that the stroke is a continuous cycle and that the new skill must be well integrated with the whole. All the same, the previous skills do not necessarily remain unaltered and they too must be reinforced frequently.

Skills are best learnt when we are free of other stresses, and so greatest success will come when we are in a stable boat having plenty of time to rehearse the action, slowly at first and then working up to full speed. On the other hand, part of the skill of rowing lies in being able to maintain (or cleverly adapt) technique in adverse wind and water conditions, and when under competitive stress and great fatigue. The skills must be learnt thoroughly first or they will break down, but many athletes do not do enough to train themselves to maintain best technique under stress. Remember, every stroke of every outing is an opportunity to improve technique, however difficult the conditions or however hard the work.

Selected technical exercises

Holding and controlling the handle

- Rowing with the inside hand only, being careful not to over-reach – change to firm pressure immediately the outside hand is replaced. This helps to give a better feel for the different roles of the two hands.
- 'Playing the piano' with the fingers during the recovery. Releases tension and shows there is no need to grip.
- Rowing with the thumbs hanging loose. Encourages a relaxed hold.
- Take off alternate hands during the recovery. Increases confidence in a relaxed hold.
- Rotate the oar in the gate during the recovery. Increases dexterity and confidence in oar handling.

Rotating the shoulders and using the outside arm

- Slide the inside hand down the loom towards the button so that the hands are a long way apart and all the work is being done with the outside hand. This exercise promotes flexibility, particularly if a special effort is made to rotate the shoulders, and will also help the proper use of the outside arm and lean towards the rigger.

The problem
Skying the blade before the catch

Possible causes
Over-reaching with the outside arm
Swinging too late on the recovery
Dropped head and curved back
Tension in hands, arms or shoulders
Dropping the hands during squaring
Balance problems.

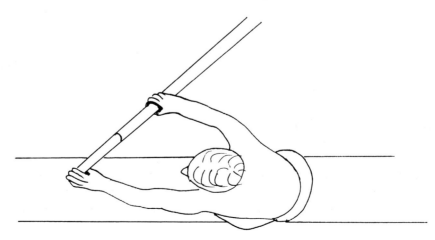

Fig. 32 Rowing with the inside hand down the loom and with exaggerated shoulder rotation

- Square blade rowing with the outside hand only is an excellent way of learning the correct outside arm action and of developing the appropriate muscles. It is difficult to balance the boat as well, so have at least two members of the crew holding the boat steady with their blades on the water.

Improving the catch

- Build up the stroke in stages of about 10–20 strokes, first using the arms only, then with body swing, ¼ slide, ½ slide and so on. These short strokes enable the catch to be very fast and at the same time improve the co-ordination of arms, back and leg drive. As the stroke progressively lengthens there should be a conscious attempt to steady the recovery and establish a good rhythm. A good variation is to build the rating smoothly at each stage and then reduce it again before moving on to the next stroke length; very high ratings and hand speeds can be achieved. Remember to stay loose and relaxed. This is also a good exercise for improving crew cohesion.

Improving the finish

- Square blade paddling. Good timing and balance is necessary to make this successful. There is a danger with this exercise of learning to cheat by washing out. The one-handed version of this, as already described, is also very valuable and many rowers perform a better finish with one hand than they do with two! The reason is usually that they tended to grip and finish with the inside hand, and probably lean away from the rigger as a result.
- Single strokes. There are many variations on this exercise but I generally prefer the pause to come at the hands-away, body-over position to encourage the correct sequence of hands, body slide; it is often valuable to increase the number of strokes between pauses progressively to help this further. Crew concentration, co-ordination and balance are also improved by these exercises.

Improving the rhythm

- Paddling at various pressures with exaggerated rhythm, i.e. with marked slide control on the recovery. This is particularly useful in conveying the idea of 'sting and float' – that is, a quick drive through the water followed by a relaxed steady pace recovery.

- Firm pressure at varied ratings. Many coaches advocate variations in rating as an additional stimulus in long-distance training, but apart from its physical effects it can also be a good way of learning how to maintain an economical rhythm despite increases in speed.
- Very low rate paddling. Maintaining a continuous stroke cycle at very low rates of striking requires great slide control and concentration on boat and oar control, and is not easy. It can be a fun way to end a hard outing!

Improving speed

- Short bursts, say 10–20 strokes, at very high speeds and ratings, with longer periods of relaxed easy paddling in between. It is best to build the speed over about 3–5 strokes before each burst and to wind down gradually after each. The emphasis must be in trying to achieve the higher speed without losing control of the blade or the rhythm, and without losing length in the water. Even in the long slog of winter endurance training, some speed work is desirable to maintain sharpness and to make the moderate ratings seem easier.

FAULT CORRECTION

Faulty technique needs to be corrected as quickly as possible, not only because it is inefficient and may affect other crew members' technique, but also because it can quickly become ingrained and then be very difficult to eradicate. Most of us will not be able to appreciate what is wrong unaided, and very often it seems easier to do it our way rather than the right way; this is where you need to listen to the coach. Before remedial action is taken, three basic points need to be checked:

1 Is the rigging right, and is it right for you?
2 Are you correctly adjusted and holding the handle well?
3 Are you fully aware of the fault and how it differs from the ideal?

Sometimes it will need the use of the video to discover what is really happening, and it is much easier to appreciate what you are doing wrong if you can see it for yourself. Often the true cause of the fault is not obvious and it is very common for problems with one part of the stroke to be derived from an earlier incorrect action. For example, a poor finish can lead to a clumsy and unbalanced recovery and in turn a poor catch. There is a school of thought which suggests that only bladework is important and bodily actions are not, but this is nonsense. The way in which the body is used to produce the blade-work and to apply power is equally important, if maximum efficiency is to be achieved. This is not to say that we need to be obsessed with irrelevant detail or with an unproductive effort to force individual athletes into a uniform mould in every tiny respect. We must also beware of the psychology of fault finding. Nobody is perfect, and constantly dwelling on what is wrong rather than emphasizing the good points is depressing and potentially demotivating. The athlete needs praise and encouragement when it does go right, even if the gain is very slight!

The list that follows cannot be exhaustive but is intended as a guide to the probable causes of some common important problems. Ideally you can then take appropriate remedial action, where necessary using a suitable selection of the exercises given previously.

The problem	Possible causes
Skying the blade before the catch	Over-reaching with the outside arm
	Swinging too late on the recovery
	Dropped head and curved back
	Tension in hands, arms or shoulders
	Dropping the hands during squaring
	Balance problems
Slow leg drive	Over-reaching or over-sliding
	Bent-arm catch or shoulder catch
	Lack of power
Blade driven too deep	Tension in hands, arms or shoulders
	Blade skyed at catch
	Poor co-ordination of legs and body
Wash-out at finish	Back curved and shoulders dropped
	Outside arm not drawing through
	Bum-shoving
	Leaning away from the rigger
	Weak upper body

Fig. 33 Washing out. The water coming from the loom shows that the blade was previously too deep

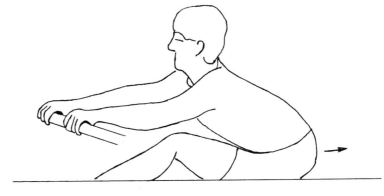

Fig. 34 Shooting the slide, or 'bum-shoving', uses up the leg drive without useful work on the handle, leaving too much for the weaker back and arm muscles to do

The problem	Possible causes
Bum-shoving	Weak upper body
	Poor co-ordination at the catch
	Over-reaching
	Curved back, dropped head
Leaning away from the rigger	Balance problems (real or imagined)
	Hands too close together
	Weak use of outside arm at finish

DIFFERENT TECHNIQUES FOR DIFFERENT BOATS

Good athletes often show the ability to be successful in any type of boat, especially if much of their early training has been in small boats. Indeed the Great Britain team crews are selected initially on their performances in small boats – a system common to many other countries. In general those who can perform well in a coxless pair will be very useful in any larger rowing boat, and the best single scullers will be good in quads and doubles, but the converse is not always true. This is not because of any dramatic difference in techniques but because the smaller boat demands greater finesse, better balance and greater adaptability. Again as a generalization, the coxed boats tend to favour larger, stronger athletes because the weight of the cox is a significant proportion of the total. The lighter and more responsive coxless boats, however, give a greater premium to power: weight ratios and technical expertise. There have been many successful examples of eights selected from the eight best scullers, but this is not a system I would favour – is your seventh best sculler necessarily better in the eight than your ninth or tenth?

The faster boats require greater speed of movement from the athlete, and the eight in particular demands a very explosive catch and leg drive and a quick, clean finish, as well as the ability to row at high ratings. The relatively heavy coxed pair and four, on the other hand, will not accelerate as quickly through the stroke and consequently the drive and draw must be particularly well sustained. Despite the different rigs that will be used on the various boat types, it is probable that the slower the boat the lower will be the most economical rating, that is, the rating that gives the best sustainable rhythm. Likewise the 4X, 4– and 8+ will respond better to bursts and sprints at much increased ratings.

Fig. 35 The essence of crew rowing is cohesion and good timing

Apart from finding someone who can steer a coxless boat and still row well (not easy for some!), the individual qualities of the athletes become important in deciding where they sit. Stroke must have an excellent rhythm, of course, but also a technique that is absolutely reliable under pressure, allied to a sense of pace and tactics, and the psychological strength to get the most out of the crew. The athlete behind must be the perfect follower and capable of imparting the rhythm to the rest of the crew. The heavies are usually in the middle of the boat (often well described as the engine room) and need to form a reliable and cohesive unit. Up in the bows the athletes should be particularly quick and responsive, not because their bit of boat is going any faster but because they are somewhat removed from the decision makers and rhythm setters in the stern. I once rowed in a four with the cox in the middle, and I found the sense of isolation in the bow half very peculiar. The same problem can arise in tandem-rigged boats where the widely separated crewmembers may find it difficult to follow stroke, and they may also have problems avoiding each other's puddles.

Although there is no doubt that technique learnt in the coxless pair or single scull is particularly valuable and, whilst such boats show up the good individual boat movers, there are some dangers in relying on them too much for selection purposes. One obvious problem lies in steering, for poor steering may gravely hamper an otherwise competent athlete. Really good pairs seem to be made in heaven and it is not always the case that two excellent rowers will make a pair that goes exceptionally fast. Other individuals or pairs may go very fast in their own idiosyncratic way and there is no certainty that they will be compatible with others in a larger boat. With the GB Juniors we have found that coxless pairs will be most valuable for identifying the most promising group of rowers, but that ultimately the decisions must rest on seat racing individuals in larger boats.

BIOMECHANICS AND ERGONOMICS – LESSONS FOR GREATER EFFICIENCY

Muscles, bones and levers

Human movement depends on a jointed skeleton acting as a system of levers, actuated by muscles pulling on the bones via tendons. In fig. 36 the superficial tissues have been removed to show the principal

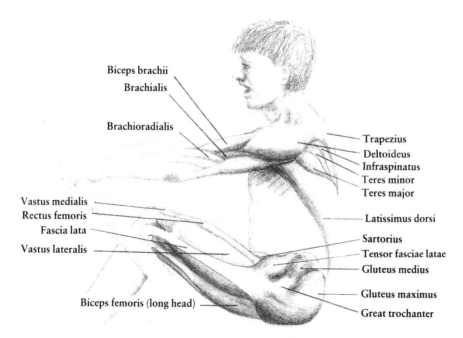

Biceps brachii
Brachialis
Brachioradialis
Vastus medialis
Rectus femoris
Fascia lata
Vastus lateralis
Biceps femoris (long head)

Trapezius
Deltoideus
Infraspinatus
Teres minor
Teres major
Latissimus dorsi
Sartorius
Tensor fasciae latae
Gluteus medius
Gluteus maximus
Great trochanter

Fig. 36 Some of the muscles used in rowing

Fig. 37 Muscles and their
skeletal attachments

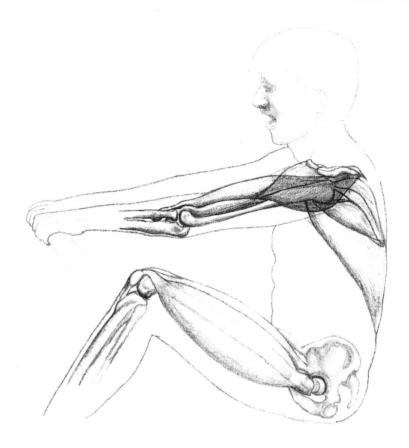

muscles involved in these actions. In truth a very much larger number
of muscles are involved, some of them contracting whilst others relax,
to produce the final controlled and co-ordinated movements – for the
sake of simplicity only the major power-producing muscles, and a few
others, are illustrated. In the next figure (fig. 37) more tissues have
been removed to show the way in which these muscles are attached to
the skeleton.

The force that can be exerted does not depend solely on the size and
activity of the muscle, but also on its length, whether it has previously
been stretched, the speed with which it is contracting, and the angles
and lengths of the bony lever system concerned. Thus the force
applied by the muscle to its insertion on a bone, and the effect it
produces, will vary through the range of movement. It is one of the
aims of good technique to exploit the best compromise of range of
movement with power.

It is important to appreciate that muscles and their associated tissues
are not just contractile units; they are also elastic, and furthermore

their contraction characteristics are related to this elasticity. This is important in a repetitive action like rowing where muscles are alternately stretched and contracted, for the effect can be exploited for greater power and efficiency of oxygen usage. Part of the increase in power is explained by what is known as the 'stretch reflex', that is, when a muscle is stretched rapidly it responds by contracting more forcefully. Another factor is the elastic energy stored temporarily in the stretched muscles and tendons, which can then be added to the next contraction. From this one can see the value of continuous motion rather than pauses during the rowing cycle so that the stored energy can be used and the muscles generate greatest force.

The angle of flexion of the knee has a very important effect in determining the speed and force of the leg drive at different stages in the stroke. We all know that it is more difficult to extend the legs vigorously when the knees are deeply flexed, whether it is rowing, weightlifting or just getting up from a low chair. In the rowing action other related principles also apply, thus the choice of knee angle is a compromise dictated by other technical requirements, including the length of stroke, and is related to the individual athlete's leg length (fig. 38). It is sometimes said that the optimum knee angle is 90 degrees and

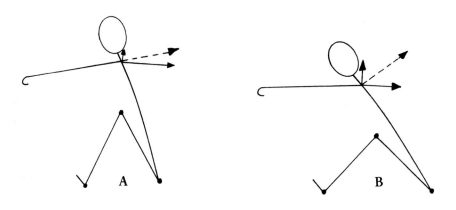

Fig. 38 Components of forces at different body positions. In B the leg muscles are not being fully utilized and energy is wasted in lifting the body

although this might be true for some weight training lifts, it has no special mechanical significance in rowing, and somewhere between 40 and 60 degrees is usual. You could of course experiment on the ergometer and find out exactly what suits you best, but then you might have to diverge from that to fit into a crew.

Since extreme knee flexion is inefficient, the argument in relation to the best compromise centres on the extent to which this loss of efficiency can be accepted, or the length of stroke made up by body swing (hence the Ratzeburg versus DDR style debate shown in fig. 28). Biomechanically it would seem that something between these two extremes is likely to give best results. The lengths of thigh and shin differ from person to person and therefore for a given stroke length the joint angles will differ between individuals. Obviously athletes with longer limbs are at an advantage because they can row the required length of stroke without using extreme joint angles. Careful adjustment of the height of the feet as well as the stretcher position can be important in establishing the optimum angles for each athlete, thus accommodating a range of leg lengths in a crew. We must be aware however that changes in the height of the feet will affect the direction in which force is applied, the body angle which can be comfortably used, and perhaps even the balance (fig. 39).

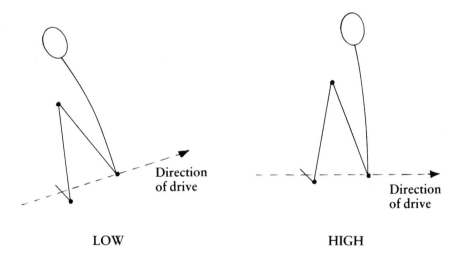

Fig. 39 The effect of the height of the feet on the biomechanics of the stroke

Direction of drive

Direction of drive

LOW

HIGH

The style that is illustrated in fig. 26 enables a rapid leg drive and allows the upper body to remain firm and to transmit the drive effectively to the handle. Early bending of the arms is not advisable during the most powerful part of the leg drive because these much weaker arm muscles will be doing unnecessary isometric work to transfer the force to the handle. Moreover, such is the nature of nervous co-ordination that early use of the arms tends to inhibit full early commitment of the legs.

Arcs and angles of the oar

Due to the fact that the oar or scull handle moves through a large arc during the stroke (about 88–93 degrees for rowing, 107–112 degrees for sculling), it is to be expected that the force applied to the handle is only at right angles to the handle, and in line with the axis of the boat, when the oar or scull is perpendicular to the boat (fig. 40).

Naturally this represents some wasted energy, but in practice the flexibility of the upper body can accommodate the changing angles to some extent, thereby devoting more force at a better angle to the handle. In sculling the flexibility of the shoulder joints takes care of it, but in rowing it is largely accomplished by rotation of the upper body, thus emphasizing the action of the outside arm. At the same time, of course, you can reach and finish much further with the outside hand. It is very desirable to pay great attention to the action of this arm, for not only must the hand travel furthest, but also that arm is in the best position for power application, especially towards the finish. Leaning slightly towards the rigger, with the outside shoulder then just a little higher than the other throughout the stroke, helps the movement. This lean will help to prevent the button being pulled away and, as we have seen, if you emphasize the inside hand you are likely to lean away and have a weak finish and balance problems.

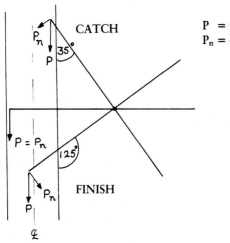

P = pull on handle
P_n = component normal to handle

Fig. 40 If the pull on the handle is along the axis of the boat then only some of the force will be at right angles to the handle

Fig. 41 In rowing it is necessary to rotate the shoulders and lean towards the rigger in order to maintain a pull at right angles to the handle and to achieve a long enough reach

The remaining question is that of the optimum angle of the oar to the boat at the catch and the finish. I suspect that we do not yet have the answer, but merely a pragmatic compromise. In fact the angles differ from one boat type to another, not for any subtle technical reason but because we use the same length oars on different rigs (more on this in Chapter 5), and few people have tried anything different. There is universal agreement however that the largest part of the total arc should be between the catch and when the oar is perpendicular to the boat. Thus for a tall crew in an eight the oar might be at 35 degrees to the boat at the catch, travel 55 degrees to the perpendicular, and then go a further 35 degrees to the finish. Four interacting things determine these angles: how far the athlete moves, the athlete's body proportions, the position of the stretcher and the rig set on the boat.

It is a biomechanical principle that the greatest work should be done in the best, most efficient, mechanical position, and this precept also applies to the arc of the oar. One purpose in starting the stroke at such an acute angle to the boat is that it inevitably takes time (and distance) for the blade to build its full grip on the water, and equally it takes time

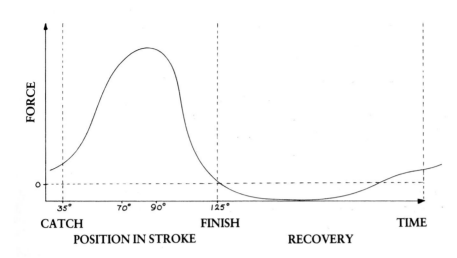

Fig. 42 Force on the pin during a complete stroke

FORCE

0

35°   70°   90°   125°

CATCH   FINISH   TIME

POSITION IN STROKE   RECOVERY

to develop full power from the muscles (fig. 42). Thus the maximum effective force on the pin is at an angle of somewhere around 70 to 90 degrees to the boat, which is where the majority of the athlete's effort is in line with the boat direction, and the blade is also at its most effective. Force on the pin reduces rapidly after this; there is no doubt that the first part of the stroke is more effective, yet the finish must maintain the acceleration of the boat. Acute catch angles, also discussed in Chapter 5, are vital in aiding the catch and rapid connection with the water.

Forces during the stroke

Forces exerted on various parts of the boat, riggers and oars or sculls can be measured by attaching strain gauges to them. Measurement of force on the swivel pin or end of the rigger is particularly relevant because it is through this point that the oar or scull drives the boat. Such studies have been very important in the development of modern rowing technique and can also be very valuable in ensuring maximum crew compatibility. A typical result such as fig. 42 shows a small step around the beginning of the stroke as the blade is accelerated into the water; if the blade enters before being accelerated sternwards then it will act as a brake and a negative force will be recorded. As the blade grips the water and begins its working arc, so the force on the pin increases rapidly. Just how rapidly depends on how quickly the athlete can mobilize maximum power. As the hands move away on the recovery, the force on the pin becomes negative and remains so until the athlete prepares for the next beginning.

Two alternative forms of the curve are shown in fig. 43. In the first (solid line), the athlete has committed full power very early; that is, before the most effective blade position has been reached. In the second (broken line), the build up of effort is more gradual and peaks later, characteristic of a slow leg drive perhaps, and part of the most effective section of the stroke is therefore underused. With modern electronics it is quite feasible to record such force/time diagrams for each athlete and thus determine the effectiveness of his or her technique objectively. It is even simpler to incorporate the necessary sensors on an ergometer (as do Rowperfect and Concept) than on a boat, and the results can be displayed in real time before the working athlete.

If the techniques of the individual crewmembers differ appreciably then there may be loss of efficiency for two reasons. Firstly the patterns of force production will not match and therefore maximum total force and speed may not be reached. Secondly, a discrepancy between bow

Fig. 43 Two different force profiles in one boat would cause the boat to snake

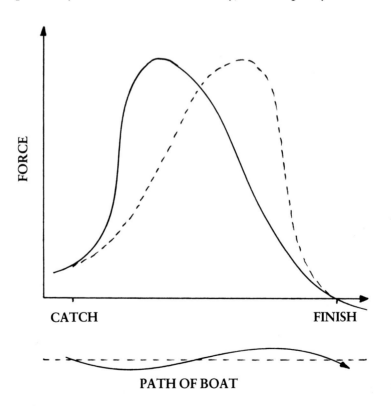

and stroke side at any point will tend to turn the boat, and this effect will be particularly noticeable early in the stroke when a large component of the blade's work is at an angle to the boat's axis. In fig. 43 two such force diagrams have been plotted together. Let us imagine that one is now characteristic of stroke, and the other bow of a coxless pair, and we can see that the boat will snake during each stroke and thus lose speed. Good pairs seem to be made in heaven!

Fig. 44 Despite their evident power, Reed and Hodge could never quite match the smoother skills of the New Zealand pair and reverted to the four at the London Olympics

4 Steering and Coxing

The ability to steer our craft exactly where we want them to go in the most efficient way is essential for three main reasons: for safety, for optimum use of our energy, and for adherence to the rules of racing. Even if one is not the crewmember in charge of the rudder it is still important that the rules and principles of good steering are understood, for there will be many occasions when we will have to give our help.

1. *Safety*   Almost invariably, whether in training or racing we are operating within confines where there is a risk of collision with other water users, with the bank or with objects in the water. In addition we are often on moving water which presents particular hazards such as weirs and turbulence or which can carry us into danger all too rapidly. Sometimes we will need to steer a particular course in order to avoid the effects of bad weather. All clubs will have their own safety rules applicable to steering and these will be in addition to the more general rules given by national associations (such as BR, as mentioned earlier) or the specific rules that apply to a particular body of water or to a particular competition. These rules must be strictly adhered to at all times.

2. *Efficiency*   Every deviation from the ideal course, or use of the rudder, represents extra distance or wasted energy and detracts from our training efforts or is a handicap in competition. A smoothly steered boat taken through the best available water on the optimum course will enjoy the best chance for the athlete to perform optimally.

3. *Racing*   In any competition there will be rules for practice and warming up on the water, approaching and attaching to the start and so on. Contravention of these rules, which are designed both

Fig. 45 Good steering is essential in regattas where each competitor must remain in their own water

for safety and the smooth running of the event, will risk disqualification. During the race itself your proper course will be defined and departure from it, even if your opponents are not hindered, may again bring the risk of disqualification.

Our boats have a natural tendency to run straight as a result of their long, slim shape, and this is greatly aided by the fin which reacts to any deviation by producing a side force (hydrodynamic lift), tending to restore the boat's course. Without the fin there might be less drag slowing the boat, but it would tend to skid about and would be unstable and difficult to keep straight. Fins are often flat plates, which work well, or can be aerofoil sections that are perhaps slightly more effective. Particularly on eights the fins can be quite deep so that they cut into less turbulent water away from the hull (see fig. 57 in the next chapter), but these have the disadvantages of being more easily damaged and sometimes too effective on a very sinuous course.

Even with a fin our boats do not always go straight because we may not pull evenly on both sides (variations in length of stroke or pressure on the blades being the most common cause), or because the boat is being moved around by water currents, waves and wash, or by the wind. At other times, of course, we do not want the boat to go straight but to follow some more elaborate direction. We therefore have to have some means of steering.

Single sculls and doubles do not require rudders because it is easy enough to steer by pulling harder, or taking a slightly longer stroke, on one side or the other. Alternatively a slightly earlier catch on one side compared to the other will do the same trick. These techniques will also help a bigger boat to negotiate sharp bends in addition to use of the rudder. It is possible to steer a pair in this way without a rudder (and I have seen it done at one World Championships) but this is rare, and all other crew boats rely on rudders to keep them on course. The rudder works by causing the stern of the boat to be pushed in the opposite direction to the deflection of the rudder. The whole boat then turns around the fin. Inevitably this process causes drag and slows the boat, so the less it is used the better. Moreover, because the rudder is below the boat it will tend to unbalance it if used clumsily. Modern

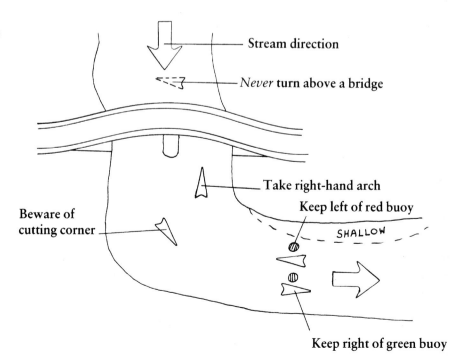

Fig. 46 Some elementary rules of the river

Stream direction

Never turn above a bridge

Take right-hand arch

Keep left of red buoy

SHALLOW

Beware of cutting corner

Keep right of green buoy

rudders are not very big and if turned through too great an angle they stall and lose effectiveness (except as a brake!). Do remember that rudders only work when they are moving through the water, and many small rudders have little effect at low speed.

Fig. 47 The Dorney Lake course used for the London Olympics has eight racing lanes and a separate channel (on the left) for warming up and access to the start. The event shown is the Oarsport Junior Sculling Head, which has a unique circulation pattern

CHOOSING YOUR COURSE IN TRAINING

As we have already seen, competitive events will have their own rules as to where you can go during training before the event and you must follow these to the letter. Some may not even let you on the water at all, and others will have particular times set aside for training. On multi-lane courses in particular, but also at other events such as Henley, there will be a well-advertised circulation pattern essential for everyone's safety (fig. 47), so you have little choice – but at other times, where should you go?

The first task is to ascertain the local rules, whether you will be on your own home water or somewhere unfamiliar. If in doubt, ask! Always check the weather and water conditions before you go afloat and find out about any particular hazards if you can. Even on your home water you must always be vigilant, for conditions change and new obstructions can occur. I once sculled into the back of the MV *Mary*, 5,000 tonnes, from Amsterdam, not because it was difficult to see but because it was moored where nothing had ever been before! During your warm-up, if you are on the same water that you are later to train or race on, look around a lot and try to memorize the land-marks and any potential obstructions or hazards.

The usual rule of the river is to keep right (as seen facing in the direc-tion of movement, i.e. starboard), although this is often modified on flowing water to keeping close to the right-hand (starboard) bank whilst going upstream, and then following the centre of the stream when coming downstream. If you are being overtaken or if you meet another craft coming the other way you should keep to the right (to starboard). If you are doing the overtaking you will normally move left (to port). Fig. 46 illustrates these normal rules of the river but you must be aware that there are often local variations, for example on the Tideway and on the River Thames at Henley other than at regatta time (when the rules will be different again!).

On a straight course with still water there are fewer problems in deciding where to go, but on flowing water the right strategy can help your steering during training and be a great advantage during a race. Going upstream you may get there sooner if you can stay suffi-ciently close to the bank to be in the slower moving water, and it is often worthwhile going a longer distance in order to achieve this. To get the full benefit you need to be very close to the bank but then you will have the added danger of hitting something, and it may not be worth taking too many chances in training (fig. 54). You will find that downstream of bridges and islands there are eddies and back-flows which might help you by breaking up the force of the stream – or they may be too unsettling and need to be avoided (fig. 48). The problem with being close to the bank or below some feature affect-ing the water is that the hull and blades may be subject to differing speeds and directions of flow. This may make the boat move about, or the blades on the two sides operate in different speeds of water. Either way this can give some very odd sensations and make the boat difficult to steer.

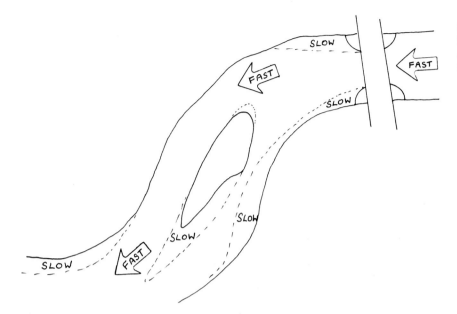

Fig. 48 Bends and obstructions in a river modify the flow and can be exploited by the steersman or sculler

As you round a bend while steering upstream there is a tendency for the bows to stick out further into the stream and, as a result, the force of the stream will tend to push the whole boat further out and make it much more difficult (sometimes impossible) to get round the bend close to the bank (fig. 49). The secret is to anticipate the problem and keep the bows tucked in as close as possible, or to start the corner from further out and then cut in as a racing car might. Sometimes it may be necessary to ease off on the inside and pull it round with the blades on the outside before the current catches the bows. A similar effect can be gained if the outside blades reach a little further for the catch than usual. If you are turning whilst facing

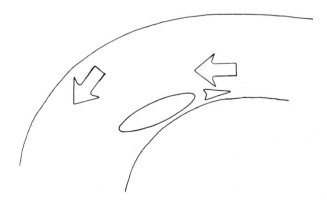

Fig. 49 On an upstream bend it pays to keep the bows out of the fastest current, or steering will be made more difficult

upstream then it is best to keep the stern near the bank and to use the faster current to swing the bows round the way you want to go. Conversely, a downstream turn works best if the bows are turned in towards the bank at the outset.

As a general rule the fastest flow downstream will be approximately in the middle of the river but with a tendency to sweep towards the outside of bends, especially at the exit (fig. 48). In a strong stream or on tight bends this latter effect can cause you to hit the bank on the exit, or at least depart from the ideal course, and it can be worthwhile cutting the corner and leaving the fastest water for a moment. There is no substitute for local knowledge but it is a good idea to watch the surface and any floating objects to get an idea of where the stream is fastest. Sometimes, as on the Tideway at low tide, you can see where the deep-water channel lies and remember this for later use, or you may be able to watch some more expert coxes or scullers and see where they steer. The ideal is to keep your boat parallel with the stream and not get across it, though it might be useful to move towards the inside of bends to take a shorter route. The other effect to think about is wind direction. An upstream wind (wind against stream/tide) will make the fastest water the roughest and there may come a time when you might choose to lose the advantage of the stream for the benefit of calmer water.

The speed of the boat relative to the water is the same whether you are going upstream or down, and the common delusion that it is harder work rowing upstream is born of the fact that it takes longer to get anywhere and the bank goes by more slowly. Close your eyes and you would not know the difference. In fact your higher absolute speed downstream means more wind resistance! Do not forget that this greater downstream speed means that it will take you longer to stop and you must allow for this if there are hazards. Every year crews and scullers (but more usually crews because it takes them longer to react and turn) get into trouble at weirs and bridges because they have underestimated the speed of the stream and how long it will take them to stop and turn. This is why we should never try to turn just upstream of a bridge (fig. 46). Remember that the current is likely to accelerate through a bridge or towards a weir, and always allow a generous margin of safety. For similar reasons it is usual practice to approach a landing in the *upstream* direction, for then the closing speed is minimized and the current can be used to bring the boat into the side. Conversely, we usually embark the same way round (i.e. *upstream*) because we can move out more easily and safely by nosing into the current at low speed, and the rudder will still have some effect.

STEERING THE SCULLING BOAT

If you have followed the advice in the second chapter your sculling boat should run straight and level most of the time and you should be able to move your hands independently of one another. Then, most of the time you will be able to steer simply by applying a little more force with one arm than the other for a stroke or two. For tighter turns many scullers make the mistake of trying to lug the boat round with a harder or longer finish. In fact it is much more effective to emphasize the catch. The best way to do this is to reach a little further with the hand on the side opposite to the way you want to turn, and then the extra reach will put the blade in nearer the bows and will help move the bows in the required direction. For very tight turns, or to spin the boat round, you may have to stop sculling and then just repeat the first part of the stroke on one side while balancing the boat or backing down on the other. The same principle applies when attached to a stake-boat (as described in Chapter 8) – use catches not finishes to get the best turning effect.

The double scull is steered in the same way, although of course you do have to be of a like mind with your partner as to which way you want to go, and it is usual for one of you to say something like 'harder with the left' if you seem to be going astray. Quads will respond to the same methods, but foot steering and a rudder usually guide these longer and faster boats and the crew continues to scull evenly except on tight turns. As in coxless fours, it is important to have one person in charge, and this is likely to be bow because of the better view forwards, even if the rudder is actually controlled from somewhere else. When racing side-by-side on a straight course there is no need for anyone to turn round, and there may be advantages in giving the job to stroke who has a clear view back down the course.

You have three points of reference for steering: the view astern, your proximity to the bank or lines of buoys, and what you can see when you look round. In training you should be in the habit of looking around a lot, perhaps every ten strokes, as much for safety as for anything else. It only takes a quick glance over one shoulder at the finish of the stroke and with practice will not affect your sculling. The banks or buoys can usually be seen well enough from the corner of your eye to give you an idea of whether you are the right distance from them, but if you are trying to follow one bank closely then it will pay to turn that way when you look round. The view astern is your best guide as to whether you are running straight, or to judge that you are turning smoothly. Focus on some point in the distance when you know that the boat is pointing in the right direction and then you can keep the stern pointing at it for as long as you want. On many straight regatta courses there are steering markers behind the start which will keep you straight when they are in line with each other.

STEERING A COXLESS BOAT WITH A RUDDER

A pair, four or quad can be steered from any position in the boat where the steering shoe is fitted, and in most boats it does not take long to change from one place to another. Traditionally, bow is the steersman because from bow you have the best view of what is coming, which may not only help steering but also be the safest. On the other hand, stroke has an absolutely clear view astern and, as in the single scull, this can be a positive advantage in maintaining a straight course. Particularly in the pair, stroke can also get a good view ahead by looking over one shoulder, and bow can be on the lookout for possible dangers, especially in training. Steering from two or three in a four is not ideal but may sometimes be necessary if the best person for the job happens to be in one of those seats. As I have already stated it is very desirable to have one person in charge and giving the orders, or at least to have a clear division of responsibilities, and in some ways it is best if that person is steering. If the boat is not bow-steered then certainly bow will need to give feedback. It is also worth remembering that in a four at speed it is bow who is most likely to be heard clearly by the rest of the crew.

For best control, it is important for the steering gear to be in good condition and well adjusted. Sit in the boat and adjust the stretcher to suit you first, then, if necessary, adjust the steering wires so that they are neither slack nor under undue tension. Check that the upper extension of the steering shoe will not foul the person in front of you when they are at backstops – if it does you may have to bend it out of the way. Get someone to hold the rudder straight while you check that the shoe is correctly aligned, i.e. at the same angle as your other foot and, if not, on most designs you can easily move the clamping position of the wires. You will also need to check that you can comfortably swing your foot to get an adequate amount of rudder both ways – in some narrow boats this may entail raising the feet or compromising on the position of the wire clamp. It is a good idea to mark the straight ahead position with something obvious like a piece of coloured tape so that you can tell easily what position the rudder is in even before you set off. The pivot on which the shoe turns is often of poor quality and may well need tightening or replacing, for otherwise it will be both difficult to row and to steer with. It is conventional for the rudder wires to be crossed so that the boat will turn the same way as you turn your foot.

As with the sculling steering described above, you have information on your course to steer from the view astern, from your position relative to the bank or buoys, and from what you can see when you glance over either shoulder. When rowing it is much easier to look over the outside shoulder at the finish (fig. 50), but you should learn

Fig. 50 A glance over the outside shoulder at the finish is usually best

to do it both ways so that you can always have a good view of what lies ahead or your distance from the nearest bank. Take a good look before you move off and if you are not giving the orders make it quite clear whether or not you are ready and it is safe to proceed. If you are giving the orders as well, as I have recommended, then make sure that you can be heard, and be clear and authoritative, for a sloppy start makes it difficult to control the boat. For those not accustomed to giving the necessary orders I suggest reading the section on coxing later in the chapter and trying to adopt some of the principles outlined there.

The coxless boat is very responsive to the rudder at high speed, but most small rudders are rather ineffective at low speeds, and if you try to turn them too much they are likely to stall and become almost useless. You need to anticipate the turn so that you can use the rudder gently but early enough. Similarly, in holding a straight course it is best to keep the boat on line by using the rudder little and often; it would be inefficient to let the boat stray off course and then have to bring it back with a large amount of rudder. Some fours tend to skid sideways and you may have to allow for this by turning into a corner a little earlier than you might otherwise expect. As explained earlier, the current on moving water can affect the way in which the boat is steered, so you need to be alert to that possibility. On tight bends or in difficult conditions you may need additional help from the crew, by getting them to ease off or hit the catches harder as appropriate. In particular, if you are bow steering you will find that you can help nudge the bows round by taking the catch a fraction earlier or with a little further reach, but beware of upsetting the balance or timing of the rest of the crew.

All this does sound rather daunting but most people soon find that, like learning to ride a bicycle, it usually falls into place with practice and then becomes more automatic. It can be difficult to think about steering and remember to row well at the same time and I would suggest that you practise first where the steering challenge is not too great. You will also find that it helps if your coach can be an extra pair of eyes and give you plenty of feedback, so that you do not have to worry too much about what might lie ahead, as well as issue gentle reminders if you stray off course. There is no doubt that experienced scullers learn more quickly because they are already used to doing their own steering and being aware of wind and water conditions – that valuable commodity known as 'watermanship'.

OUTINGS IN THE DARK

Many crews and scullers have to train in the dark, particularly in the winter, and far from being unpleasant this is often the best time of day, when the wind has dropped and the pleasure boats have gone away. Nevertheless rowing or sculling in the dark or in poor visibility is dangerous and is not to be encouraged. It is rarely completely dark on most rowing courses in Britain because even when the sky is cloudy there is stray light from buildings and street lights, and the water reflects what light there is. Once your eyes have become fully accustomed to the dark (which might take up to half an hour), you can see quite well enough to steer, but you must already be very familiar with the course in the light. Do check in advance what other boats are likely to be out at the same time, be extra vigilant and observant, and be certain to keep to the local rules of the river or course. Do not go out if it is foggy, if there is a fast stream, or if there is a danger of hitting driftwood or ice. All boats used at night must carry lights, which include a bright white light shining forward and aft, and which can be seen through 360 degrees, and, in addition, must meet any special requirements of the local water authority. Coaching launches used at night must meet the required lighting regulations and must carry a powerful waterproof torch with all the rest of the prescribed safety gear. If the coach is on the bank they should also have such a torch and there should be one in the boat.

STEERING IN RACES

In most cases heads give you enough room for a choice of steering strategies as well as enough space for overtaking, although there may be some restrictions of which you will be advised. The organizers may also give other steering advice as well as the specific instructions for marshalling before the start (fig. 51), the start procedure, and what to do after the finish. Memorize these instructions – some people also take them with them in the boat.

The object of marshalling is to get all the competitors in order and in place out of the way of the racing course well before the race start. For some big events the marshalling is a very complex multi-stage operation and it is essential that you are on time and very co-operative with the officials. Often you will have to turn before the start

Fig. 51 Marshalling for the
start of a major head

and you need to think about how you are going to do that so as to
get yourself into the best position – not always easy in a strong
stream. Your aim should be to give yourself plenty of room in which
to build up to racing speed on exactly the right course before the
timing line.

Find out as much as you can about the course and its vagaries before
you race and apply the principles outlined earlier for dealing with
upstream or downstream racing (fig. 48). If you have the choice do not
start too close to the boat ahead to ensure that you have clean water
and also enough space to manoeuvre if you find yourself catching it
early on. In most events there are strict rules for overtaking which will
include making way for faster boats, but from your point of view you
do not want to deviate far from the ideal racing line whether you are
doing the overtaking or the opposite. However, it is unforgivable to
deliberately impede a faster crew. At the finish try not to slow abruptly
or turn in front of following boats, but be on the lookout for crews
ahead of you that might be doing just that.

The Tideway course – variously used for the Oxford and Cambridge race, the Head of the River Race, Women's Eights Head, Schools Head, Pairs Head and the Fours Head – is a special challenge. When the tide is strong the water flow can be very fast and this makes marshalling and turning quite tricky. The water level can also drop quickly and every year boats risk being grounded and damaged. The apparent width of the course lures many competitors into leaving the fairly narrow optimum racing line, whilst so often its wind and waves present the dilemma of sticking to that line or aiming for more shelter. Staying in the fastest moving water (roughly on the deep water line) makes such a difference that everyone steering this course should make every effort to learn it.

Side by side or multi-lane racing on a straight still water course should present the minimum of steering problems – you just have to go straight down the middle of your lane. In practice it may not be quite so easy because the lanes may be quite narrow and you can, for example, be blown off course by a crosswind. If you trespass onto someone else's water or risk a collision the umpire should warn you and tell you to move to port or starboard (left or right), but if you do not respond, interfere with another crew's progress, or gain some unfair advantage, then you risk disqualification. If the lanes are well buoyed then you will find it fairly easy to tell if you are on course, but I have raced on some continental lakes where there were very few buoys and had to use distant markers such as a church spire to plot my course.

In side-by-side races on moving water and/or a winding course you may be able to gain some legitimate advantage with creative steering to straighten the bends or avoid, or make best use of, the stream as described earlier. Sometimes, particularly if the lanes are not buoyed, it may be possible to gain an advantage over your opponents without actually encroaching on their water. If you have the inside of the bend it is legitimate to approach the bend as wide as possible to ensure that they have to go the long way round. If you turn in late, this not only hoids out your opponents but also moves you forward in relation to the other boat. It is called 'making a corner' (fig. 52). If the umpire is following in a launch then the launch should be in the middle of the course and this can be a very useful guide for the sculler or steersman of a coxless boat.

Some courses are notoriously difficult to steer and oddly enough this includes the straight Henley one, where the penalties include not

Fig. 52 Making a corner gives the crew on the inside a great advantage

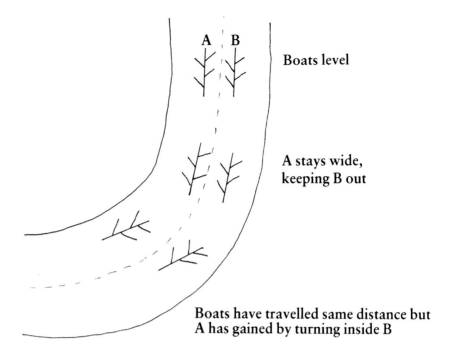

A   B

Boats level

A stays wide, keeping B out

Boats have travelled same distance but
A has gained by turning inside B

only the sanctions of the umpires, but also the potential disaster of hitting the wooden booms lining the course. Here the problem is that although the course is straight the river is not, and consequently the stream pushes the boat sideways in different ways at different places. Added to this are the very patchy wind shadows created by the large trees along the banks, and the fact that the course varies substantially in its distance from the bank. In some years the stream is strong enough to disadvantage the Bucks station, particularly near the finish, but that is the luck of the draw and the course is too narrow to avoid it.

COXING

The cox should be much more than just the person who steers the boat. He or she should also be the person in charge throughout the training outing or race, who makes the crew perform as a unit, gets the best from them, gives them all the feedback they need on what is happening around them, while at the same time being the coach's on-board mouthpiece. Anyone who doubts the cox's involvement in the crew's success, even at the highest level, should look at the pictures of a tear-streaked and emotional Gary Herbert on the rostrum after he and the Searle brothers had won the coxed pairs at the Barcelona Olympics. To do all this successfully requires much skill and a strong personality, but commonly the cox starts with the disadvantage of being the smallest in the crew and sometimes also the youngest and least experienced. The cox is also the one whose mistakes are noticed by everyone else and who tends to be the butt of jokes and a scapegoat for misfortune. Nevertheless, this is the person who has enormous responsibility and power, who can make all the difference in a race and can win the respect and affection of the crew. Unfortunately, the cox is often the one member of the crew who gets the least coaching and practical tuition but who needs it as much as anybody – so I make no apologies for getting right down to basics in this section.

Before you start you must consider the question of safety, for this is of paramount importance both for you personally and for the crew for which you will have responsibility. You must be able to satisfy your club's safety advisor and the crew's coach that you are healthy and have adequate vision and hearing. If you suffer from epilepsy, black-outs, or have any other medical condition that might at any time affect your control of the boat, then your coach and the crew should be aware of the action to take should a problem arise. You should be able to swim well enough to cover at least 50 metres in light clothing (or meet the possibly more demanding rules of your club). However, BR suggests that if there is some reason why you are unable to meet this requirement then you could still cox wearing the obligatory lifejacket. All coxswains must wear an approved lifejacket at all times when on the water, and inflatable ones must not be worn under other clothing. You must ensure that you know how to use the lifejacket and that you will be able to escape easily from the boat whilst wearing it (really only a possible problem with 'front-loader' boats). You must wear adequate warm and waterproof clothing in cold weather, but you should beware of wearing items which will hinder your movement or which could be a problem if you fall in.

All this and more are in the Water Safety Code (issued by BR in Great Britain) and you must ensure that you are familiar with that as well as the special rules of your own club. You have a responsibility for not only the safety of your boat and crew but also that of other water users and you will have to be vigilant and learn competence in boat handling. If this sounds daunting be reassured that most of it is just good common sense and lots of youngsters quickly learn to be very accomplished, and that our sport is really a very safe one.

It is important for a new cox to appreciate that the crew want and need someone in charge. Even the most experienced crews would prefer to concentrate on their rowing and leave the boat handling up to you. They want someone who knows what to do, and who tells them what they have to do. Inexperienced crews are in even greater need of a leader and will flounder without firm guidance. Thus your first priority apart from safety and correct steering is to learn the orders you must give to make things happen, and the second is to learn how to give them in such a way that they inspire confidence and are quickly obeyed.

Let us follow through the series of operations and orders that you might use in a typical outing and see how they should work. Before you do anything else, though, make sure that you are ready, in that you are appropriately dressed (see Chapter 9) and have everything you need such as microphone, amplifier, stopwatch and perhaps a small toolkit. Listen to the coach as the crew is briefed and make sure that you know exactly what is going to happen during the outing – if necessary writing down the key things you will have to do. I think it is also the coxswain's job to get the blades out and put in a safe but accessible position ready for the crew, but clubs vary in their system for this. You may well be given responsibility for checking that they are correctly adjusted.

Getting the boat out

First make sure that you have the whole crew assembled and then say clearly and firmly, 'Hands on the boat'. It may be necessary to tell them where they should stand, for example, 'Opposite your riggers', if it is a rowing boat upside down on its rack with both sides accessible. More usually only one side of the boat is clear and the crew will have to lift it off the rack and half of them hold it while the others duck underneath. Most boathouses are very crowded and it is vital not to damage the boat, so it will often be necessary to remind the crew to, 'Mind the rack/riggers above', or some such. They may also have to edge the boat out on the half turn, and it will be your job to tell them when to do this, and when to turn the boat level again. You should work all this out in advance so that there is no delay or confusion when you come to it. If you are not sure what to do, then ask someone who does. At some stage, perhaps not until you are outside you must also make it plain whether you want the boat carried on their shoulders or at waist height – you will only need a single order, 'Shoulders', or, 'Waists'.

Getting the boat on the water

You must know in advance which way the boat must face when you put it on the water (on moving water this will usually be with the bows pointing upstream so that you will have the best control when you move off), and if necessary turn the boat round *before* you reach the pontoon/landing stage. When you are in place it will have to be turned over and placed carefully on the water, and it is your job to ensure that this is done in a co-ordinated way without risking damage to the hull. An experienced crew will lift the boat above their heads, step back in line, lower it to their waists and then place it on the water. Your orders would be, 'Throwing the boat, stroke side (or bow side, as appropriate) under; one, two, three, up! And lower; on the water!' Inexperienced or weak crews will not be able to do this and will have to use the more undignified procedure of first turning the boat, then one side holding it while the others scramble underneath, before placing the boat on the water. While all this is happening you should be standing at one end of the boat facing the crew so that they can hear your orders clearly. As soon as the boat is on the water you must hold it firmly, probably best by a rigger towards the bows, and if there is wind or stream pull the bows in towards the pontoon so that it cannot swing out.

Getting the crew in the boat

The crew will need to fetch their blades while you hold the boat, but if there is a strong stream or it is windy you should get some of the crew to help you hold the boat. Meanwhile you can put your cox-box in place and check that it works. Blades on the side nearer the raft should be put in their gates and the others placed across the boat – an experienced crew may not need orders for this. With rowing boats it is then usual for those rowing on the side nearer the raft to hold the riggers while the other side step in and put their blades in their gates. Only when the gates are done up should you allow the side holding the riggers to get in. Hold on tight to a rigger – it will be your fault if they fall in! If you were coxing a quad or an octuple you would tell the bow pair or the bow four to step in first. The reason for boating just half the crew at a time is for safety when it is potentially very unstable. The orders would be, 'Stroke side (or bow side) hold the riggers, bow side (or stroke side) in! Blades out! Do up the gates!' Then, when you can see that all is ready, you order the others in. Continue to hold a rigger while all this is happening and while the crew settles in and adjusts, and then have a roll call from bow to check that everyone is ready. Tell the crew to hold onto the raft while you get in but try to be quick.

Moving off

You will have made yourself aware of any rules, regulations, hazards, safety precautions and so on well in advance and you should have found out from the coach or crew what you are going to do during the outing. Have a good look round, and when you are ready tell the crew to push off from the raft. Sometimes you may have deliberately boated quickly to clear the pontoon for other crews and your own crew may not be ready to row, but it is preferable to get them paddling straight away so that your rudder becomes effective. It is often best to just use the bow pair or four at this early stage while the rest of the crew sit the boat level. Often rowing with just part of the crew is a useful part of the warm-up. You should know what sort of warm-up procedure the crew is expecting or the coach may instruct you. It is right that you should be in charge of the boat and that you relay the instructions to the crew, and they must do as you tell them.

The common orders you will have to give will be of the sort: 'Come forward (or your crew may be used to starting from 'Backstops'); paddling light/half pressure/ firm, etc.; are you ready? Go!' If you want to make a change while the crew is in motion it is best to warn them with, 'Next stroke, paddle firm/light (or whatever)'. When on the move your orders must not only be loud, clear and incisive, but should also fit in with the rhythm of the stroke so that the end of the order coincides with the finish of the stroke. To stop the boat you say, 'Easy all!' (or 'Way enough!' If you are American). The crew should balance the boat with the blades clear of the water until you give the order to lower or drop them. If you want to stop, the order is, 'Hold her up!' or 'Hold her lightly' for a gentle stop. In an emergency, shout 'Hold her hard!' For turning you can use the momentum of the boat by saying 'Hold her stroke side (or bow side)', and the boat will turn that way. You can continue the turn by getting the other side to paddle on. If you want the boat to turn more sharply, when it has come to a halt, then tell one side to alternate paddling forwards with the other side backing down – the boat will then spin more or less in its own length.

Be determined not to tolerate any poor or tardy responses by your crew and to maintain your control, however senior your crew. It is in their interest as well and if you show that you expect high standards they will respect you for it.

Steering

After reading the first part of this chapter you will know the general principles of steering, but above all you must be safe on the water. This means thinking ahead, following all the safety rules, and keeping a good lookout for other water users and potential hazards, such as swimmers! The aim of good steering is always to know where you are going well in advance and to go there in the smoothest way possible, keeping your boat on line all the time and using as little rudder as possible. Boats do differ in the way in which they respond, depending on the shape and size of the hull, fin and rudder, but in all cases use of the rudder slows the boat and may affect its balance. Applying the rudder when the blades are in the water will have least effect on the balance. Most boats skid outwards on bends taken at speed and you may have to allow for this by starting your turn a little earlier. As shown in fig. 49 you need to keep the bows well tucked in on upstream bends or the current will tend to push you wide. You crew will not appreciate having to row against the stream unnecessarily so try to keep out of the worst when going against it, and on the other hand they will appreciate a cox who keeps them in the best water going down (see fig. 48).

If you are in a stern-coxed boat, particularly an eight, you probably cannot see much straight ahead, so you will have to have a quick look either side at frequent intervals. Do not lean out when you do this because it is likely to upset the balance, and it is best to do it while the blades are in the water. You should always settle yourself firmly in your seat both to give yourself a more comfortable ride and to minimize your effect on the balance. Sydney Olympic champion Rowley Douglas developed a model style where he tucked himself in his cockpit to lower his centre of gravity and minimize wind resistance. Fig. 53 shows the GB Junior cox Syd Hayes doing everything he could to help his crew to their bronze medal. Some padding behind your back is also a good idea so that you can sit back in the seat and not get bruised by the jolting. In a rear-coxed boat you can help the balance by bracing your legs against the side of the cockpit or pushing against the footboard.

In a front-coxed boat ('front loader') you have a much better view ahead, of course, but it is harder to judge your width at first and may be a little harder to tell if you are going straight. You are also somewhat out of touch with your crew and what they are doing, and it is much more difficult to be aware of what is happening behind your boat – whether you are being overtaken for example. It is very important that

Fig. 53 The cox has a key part to play in encouraging the crew and informing them about their opponents. Note how the British cox (lane 4) is keeping as low as possible in the boat

you can get out easily from a front loader in the unlikely event of a capsize, and you must make sure that neither your clothing nor your equipment, such as your lifejacket, will impede you. If you do have to get out in a hurry stay calm and relaxed, don't struggle with your legs, but put your hands on the rim of the cockpit and lift yourself out by levering with your arms and leaving your legs trailing.

Talking to the crew

As you gain in experience of the sport, and listen to other coxes and to what your coach says to the crew, you will learn what to say and when. Ask the crew what they particularly want you to say and make sure that you are in touch with what the stroke is trying to do. In selecting coxswains for the GB Junior teams we not only look at their boat handling and steering but seek feedback from their crews, and we also listen in to them with a radio, or even tape record them in action. It might be a good idea to listen to a recording of yourself and go through it with your coach, for we often don't really appreciate how we sound to others.

You need to be positive, constructive and not a nag, and avoid too much repetition. Look out for the technical points that the coach has made and remind the crew of those from time to time, but don't interrupt while the coach is talking. Give the crew information that they need such as rating or number of minutes elapsed in a training piece. If the crew is working hard then be encouraging and confident, sometimes even aggressive and demanding; if they are not doing so well it is better to say things like: 'We can do better than that, let's really go for it next time,' rather than be abusive. Do not feel that you have to talk non-stop; if you do, after a while the crew will cease listening.

Coming back in

At the end of the outing, and indeed at the end of any piece of hard work, you must allow your crew to wind down rather than stop abruptly. The outing should conclude with a few minutes of light and relaxed paddling as you approach the landing stage. This also allows you to make a slow and controlled landing and judge when to stop paddling so that you can glide the last few metres at minimal speed with the boat balanced and the blades raised. Remember that we usually come in against any stream even if it means going past and turning. It looks very neat if you steer in towards the raft edge at first and then use the rudder to turn away at the last moment. The boat will then slide in sideways as it comes to a halt. Make sure that you are disentangled from things like microphone leads, and as soon as the boat is docked leap out and grab a rigger to hold the boat steady.

The safest procedure for disembarking the crew is the most disciplined one, in strict order:

1 Tell the side nearer the stage to get out together and then to hold their riggers
2 Order: 'Blades out everyone!'
3 Now tell the rest of the crew to get out: 'One foot, out, together!'

With a sculling crew you have to do it differently. You could get the whole crew out together after they have undone their gates, but this leaves just you holding a rigger to prevent a capsize. It would be better to get some of the crew out first to help you hold the boat.

The crew can now put their shoes on and put the blades aside while you continue to hold the boat. Lifting the boat out of the water must be done with care and it is a good idea to tell the crew to put one hand under the boat so that they do not scrape it against the edge. When the crew are in position you would tell them, 'Hand across, one hand under, are you ready, lift!' The expert crew will once again throw the boat, one side moving across, before lowering it to the carrying position, but only you should give the orders. Novices will have to repeat the procedure of half the crew holding the boat while the others duck under before they can turn the boat and carry it. Do make sure that you have the boat pointing the right way before you enter the boathouse – it would be so embarrassing to have to come out again!

The cox is a vital part of the crew and it is a very responsible job. If you are not sure what to do then do ask for help and advice, particularly from your coach but also from key members of the crew. Remember that your performance is as important as theirs is. It pays to make yourself useful in other ways too, and if you are the one who checks that boat and blades are in good condition and properly adjusted before the outing, and you are the one who remembers what is to be done during the outing, then you will earn their respect and improve their performance in your charge. There is no doubt that every cox should learn how to scull at least, and to row if possible, so that they know at first hand what it is all about. You should not neglect your own need for exercise either, and who knows, if you grow too big for coxing you could become a first-class rower yourself, as many have done before you.

COXING IN RACES

Before you go racing look again at the section earlier in this chapter concerning steering in races, and also read Chapter 8 so that you understand the process from the crew's point of view. Of course, your main duty is to get them safely to the start on time and then steer the best course to the finish, but a good cox can do so much more than this and really can win the race for the crew.

First of all, make sure that both you and your crew are absolutely clear as to the arrangements and timing for the race and, if you are not staying together, exactly when and where you are to meet. Before the race you must find out as much as possible about the course and the conduct of the race, and this includes how to get to the start and where you can do your warm-up. Check over the boat and blades, making

Fig. 54 Steering close the bank in an upstream head race saves precious time. The cox must, however, be on the lookout for obstructions!

sure that every nut and bolt is tight and also that you have all your coxing equipment and that it works. In regattas you will almost certainly be weighed, sometimes before a specified time, but not usually for heads. You will probably be given a weight certificate that you must keep with you in case an official wants to check it before or after the race. Make sure that you will be above the minimum weight, if necessary carrying a suitable makeweight. You must present yourself for weighing in the clothes you will wear for the race including your lifejacket, but not your cox-box, which is deemed to be part of the boat. Any makeweight you carry will be checked and must not be attached to you but stowed safely close to you in the boat – it may be checked again at any time, including after the race.

The minimum weight for coxswains is currently: 55 kg for Senior Open, Veteran Open, J18, J16 and mixed crews; 50 kg for Senior women, Veteran women, WJ18 and WJ16 crews; 45 kg for all J15 and younger crews. In domestic events any amount of dead weight may be carried but it is restricted for international events.

Try to keep an eye on whether the event is running to time, but do not assume that your own race will necessarily be delayed. See what sort of queue there is for getting on the water and whether there is any hold-up for checking boat safety – make sure that you allow plenty of time. Check that the correct numbers have been collected and attached to you, the boat and the crew as necessary. Keep calm, for the crew will be getting edgy and the more people around them who are calm and sensible the better. Ensure that your blades will be easily to hand when you boat so that you do not hold up others, and it is usually courteous to push off as soon as possible and complete your crew's adjustments on the water. Be very vigilant as you go to the start or warm-up area, making sure that you follow the organizers' rules, because you may not have much room and there will be lots of other craft on the water. You should have worked out in advance what you are going to do in the warm-up and where, but you may have to show some flexibility and initiative in this. Do be very careful; I have seen many accidents where crews are trying to warm up in a restricted space; do not assume that other crews know what they are doing. You must also keep a very careful eye on the time so as to ensure that you arrive at the start or marshalling area in good time.

For a head race there will be a marshalling system which you must know before you go afloat. Standards of marshalling vary considerably and you may be very well directed to your correct place, or have to find it for yourself – it is usually not difficult to work it out if you know where you should be relative to other competitors. You may be told when to get ready to move off towards the start, so that your crew can remove extra clothing, and when to move to the start – but sometimes you just have to guess from what other crews ahead of you are doing. Stay calm and alert, keep your crew informed and turn cleverly onto the start as described earlier. You should be a sensible distance behind the crew in front, if you are not leading off, and you must judge where to get your crew up to race speed so that you cross the timing line at full speed. There are usually at least a few strokes between the start signal and the timing line.

Help your crew to settle into its pre-arranged race plan, and all the way over the course inform them where they are and whether they are holding to the correct pace. Try to do this in an encouraging way – not by emphasizing what a long way they still have to go! Do keep an eye on what is happening behind you (not easy in a front loader and you may have to arrange for one of the crew to help you) and, if necessary, move out of the way of a faster crew smoothly and with the minimum loss before regaining your optimum course. Tell your crew if you are catching ones in front and keep them informed as you overtake. Make sure that the other crew know that you are there and if possible stick to your course and expect them to move, but not at the expense of a collision. From time to time remind your crew of key technical points and try to praise their efforts; this will help to distract them from their feelings of fatigue. As you approach the finish you should be sounding even more upbeat and excited, and with a minute or so left you will be driving the crew to go all out for the finishing line. Make sure you know exactly where it is, do not wind down until the whole boat has crossed the line, and do not stop but paddle on until you are clear of the line.

In a regatta you will again have to get your crew to the start safely and in good time. You must be at the start and ready to race (i.e. lined up in race direction, and attached to the starting pontoon or stake-boat if they are being used) at least two minutes before race time. In a free start you have to ensure that you are in the right position in your lane and in no danger of clashing with your opponent. If you are not ready, or unhappy with your position, put your hand up so that the starter can see it. For a stake-boat start you must back onto the stake-boat or pontoon very carefully and then keep the boat straight. Always try to get your crew ready and your boat in line as soon as possible so that

you cannot be taken by surprise by a sudden start. Keep your hand up
all the time that you are not ready, and then when you are ready tell
the crew, 'Hand coming down'. In multi-lane racing there is a call-over,
naming each crew in turn, and in side-by-side racing the starter will
also name each crew, it is then up to you to be ready and stay ready,
and the start could come at any moment even if you had your hand up
(see Chapter 8).

From the start it is important for you to remind the crew what they
should be doing as they accelerate and then settle into their race pace.
The tactics for the race will have been pre-arranged and you must not
forget them, but you may also have to react to changing circumstances. It is vital that you stay in your water throughout the race and
do not risk disqualification, but if you are warned for your steering
make sure that you respond promptly. You will be able to see how you
are progressing relative to your opponents but until your crew is
settled after the start keep their minds on what they are doing; later,
keeping them informed means they will be less tempted to look
around. During the race you need to be loud and positive but varying
the tone of your voice and what you say to cater for your crew's needs.
Calm and steady them if they tend to rush, drive them aggressively
when necessary, and whip them up for a last dash for the line if you
need to. Keep aware of your opponent's moves and be prepared to
respond quickly if necessary.

Fig. 56 On a multi-lane course
the cox must keep strictly in
lane and also monitor the
position of the other crews

5 Boat and Oar Design, Construction and Rigging

Every athlete should understand their equipment so that they may make the best choice from what is available, be able to use it in the best possible way, and know the importance of looking after it well. In our sport, understanding the principles of the design and construction of the equipment also helps you to adopt the techniques that make the best use of it. Modern boats are very adjustable but it takes more than just a knowledge of how to make the adjustment in order to get the best result – you should also appreciate what effects a change might have, and why. Boats and blades are delicate and expensive and all users must realize the importance of maintaining them in first-class condition. Many readers may have to make their own repairs and modifications and will need to know something of the materials and methods of boat construction. Similarly many of you will be involved in decisions about which boats or blades to buy.

RESISTANCE TO MOVEMENT THROUGH WATER

As briefly described in Chapter 1, the movement of a boat through water encounters two kinds of resistance or drag: the energy transferred to waves made by the hull, and the energy transferred to the water by friction against the hull surface. These sources of drag are both affected by the displacement of water by the boat in order to float, and by the speed. The displacement, as Archimedes told us, depends on the combined mass of the crew, boat and ancillaries, and larger displacements will mean increased wave drag. At the same time the larger displacement will present a greater wetted surface and will therefore experience more friction drag. For any given crew weight, then, it is desirable that the boat and its ancillaries are as light as possible, and

Fig. 57 The V-shaped waves from the bows and stern of this eight can be seen, as well as the turbulent wake left by the friction of the hull against the water

that its shape is the best compromise that will make the smallest waves and have the smallest wetted area. All-up weight makes a difference in several ways, as was shown in Chapter 1, so it does make sense to keep it to a minimum.

As a general rule for the long narrow boats that we use, and within the usual speed range, the wave drag is the smaller of the two resistances. The exact proportions are difficult to estimate precisely and in any case vary with the class and speed of boat. Extensive testing is far too expensive for the rowing world but some tank tests have been carried out, and sailing catamarans have similar slim hulls and have been more thoroughly researched. The results show that wave drag does not increase with speed in an even fashion, but it does increase very rapidly at higher speeds, especially when the bows are creating a crest and the stern a trough. The boat is then going uphill! Eventually it reaches a critical speed known as 'hull speed', and so much energy would be needed to exceed it that it effectively limits the speed of a human-powered displacement craft. With an engine, hull speed can be beaten by planing or by using hydrofoils.

As far as wave drag is concerned, a minimal value will be achieved if the faster boats are longer, which is generally the case. There are also critical wave speed interactions with the bottom of the watercourse and this means that in, for example, the 2–3 metres shallow water of many artificial courses; shorter eights have a slight advantage, whereas longer eights have a distinct advantage in deep water. Calculation suggests that the long, narrow, finely pointed boats with which we are familiar are already close to the optimum shape. In any case practical considerations are important; for example, some short hulls are very narrow at cox and bow seats. One way of overcoming this problem is to widen the saxboards, and parallel-sided boats not only provide room for wide hips but also enable the riggers to fit anywhere. Bearing in mind that wave drag is the smaller proportion of the total, it would seem that the possible gains from new shapes will be small, but they might be critical for success.

Friction drag is largely governed by the area of wetted surface, the smoothness of that surface and the viscosity of the water, as well of course by the speed through the water. Approximately, the friction drag increases as the square of the speed, and the power required by the cube, and this is why even small increases of speed are so costly in effort. A rounded short boat like a coracle will have a small surface area but its wave drag would be unacceptable. For a longer hull a

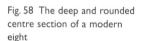

Fig. 58 The deep and rounded centre section of a modern eight

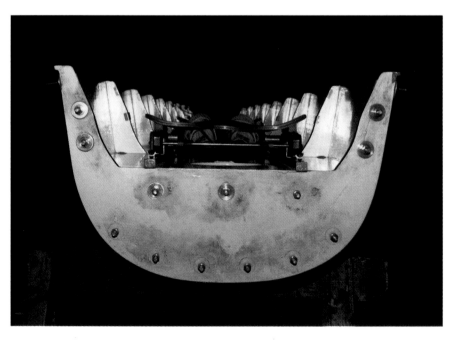

semicircular cross-section under water will give the minimum surface area to volume ratio, but this needs to change to a parabolic or vee section for best surface cutting at the bows. The width of the hull and the way in which it tapers not only affects the way in which the water flows over the surface but also affects its stability. A wider, shallower section boat will be more stable for the novice, but even the elite can find that very fine boats are too tricky to allow them to give of their best (fig. 59).

Fig. 59 Cracknell and Pinsent struggle to control their pair on lumpy water at Henley

Surface finish is critical. Any roughness can make the water flowing over the surface (the boundary layer) turbulent and will increase drag. A completely smooth painted or plastic finish is best, and it must be kept clean and free from scratches. Many claims have been made for specialized friction-reducing finishes but extensive testing by the yachting fraternity has failed to find any that work. Wax or silicone polishes are not desirable since the hull will not be wettable and the boundary layer may separate; instead it is common practice to wash the hull with detergent before racing to ensure the best surface. There are some polymers that will affect the properties of water in a way that greatly affects friction, but such substances have long been banned by FISA. FISA also acted swiftly to outlaw the application of polyester micro-grooved film to the hull, an offshoot of the America's Cup campaigns, but one that owed its origins to research into the remarkable properties of dolphin skin and its possible use on submarines. There are some slimy microbes that cause problems in testing tanks – perhaps we could grow those on our boats. Lastly there is the undoubted advantage of warmer water and its lower viscosity. The difference can be substantial, commonly amounting to 2–3 lengths for an eight over 2,000 metres between winter and summer in England.

Official weighing of boats at FISA championships shows that boats from a large number of different makers fall well within 10% of the FISA limits – some even have to carry ballast. Similar boats do differ a little in weight, as is to be expected from hand-made products, and they may absorb and lose small amounts of water as well (fig. 60). Since little can be done to make lighter boats this has led to an intensification of the search for better hull shapes or other advantages. Although little data is available from precise tank testing it would be foolish to ignore the self-evident qualities of the winning boats. Whilst the crew or sculler may be the most important factor, champions do not choose slow boats and in many cases they have arrived at their choice after careful trials of several different boats, or may have had

Fig. 60 Boats roast in the sun in Zagreb. Some will lose weight, as absorbed moisture is lost, others may be in structural danger

the boat specially made for them. In fact, championship results indicate that several makes are likely to show very similar performance, which is not so surprising when some of them are copies of the same design. So, perhaps the choice may be made more on grounds of national loyalty, individual preference, or cost.

AIR RESISTANCE

Because of the low air speeds and apparently small forces involved, not much attention has been paid to the importance of air resistance (aerodynamic drag) in retarding the boat. A figure of about 10% of the total drag from all sources is commonly guessed at. If true this is actually highly significant, and if one bears in mind that a headwind can easily double the air speed experienced by the boat without making the water unrowable, then it is not surprising that headwinds have such a dramatic effect on race times. The possibility of strong winds during the Olympic regattas of both Sydney and Athens certainly made many coaches consider what they could do to reduce the effect.

There is no doubt that a well-fitting rowing suit and short hair reduces the athlete's wind resistance significantly, and it is also possible to reduce the drag caused by the equipment. A coxswain lying prone in the bows not only lowers the centre of gravity but keeps the cox out of the airflow, and although this option is not permitted for eights the cox can crouch as low as possible and keep arms and elbows within the saxboards. The slimmer looms of carbon oars reduce their drag by 35% compared with the old fashioned wooden ones, and the aerofoil section riggers that have been used (and which doubtless could be made even 'cleaner') are also advantageous. Further gains have also been made in smoothing the shape of the above-water parts of the boats (fig. 61).

BOAT CONSTRUCTION

The design requirements that the racing boat must satisfy are now well established. The boat must be strong enough of course to withstand the forces exerted on it by its crew and the wind and water. It must be as light as the rules allow, and at the same time the boat must be stiff enough to withstand the applied loads without appreciable distortion.

Fig. 61 Wing riggers stiffen the structure at a critical point and enable conventional shoulders to be omitted. Other forms of rigger may have aerodynamic advantages. The hull is a high-performance composite of carbon fibre and plastic foam bonded with epoxy resin

Just how stiff is a matter of debate, for a very stiff boat feels harsh and may be difficult to row even though it does not waste energy by distorting with strain, whereas a flexible boat can be hard to balance as well and loses energy and speed. The hull must have an excellent exterior finish and must be shaped to give the best compromise between minimum wave drag and friction drag. The above-water parts should be shaped so that aerodynamic drag is reduced. Finally the configuration of the boat and the details of its internal construction must afford the athletes the most efficient working positions and allow the oars or sculls to be optimally placed.

The greatest stresses imposed by the athletes on the structure are principally on the foot stretchers and the outrigger attachment points, and these are the parts that most commonly fail under repeated stress. These local forces are likely to be in the order of 50–100 kg in sustained rowing (but will be much greater at the start), and those parts of the structure must indeed be strong to withstand repeated strain. The general forces on the hull are of a much lower order however. The hydrostatic pressure on the hull in supporting the boat plus crew will be only about 200 kg/m^2 and very thin skins can withstand that providing they are otherwise supported against distortion (for example with ribs, or by sandwich construction). The thin skins of the materials commonly in use will also be quite adequate for the tensile strength of the hull. 'Wing' riggers can not only offer aerodynamic advantages if properly designed but offer structural advantages. Particularly in sculling boats they enable the shoulders to be done away with, which saves weight and gives more room for the hips, and if the wing connects the two sides of the boat it greatly stiffens it (fig. 61).

It is not difficult to make a strong, stiff, heavy boat, but it is difficult to make a light boat that is both adequately strong and stiff. By and large the final consideration in choosing materials and construction for a light boat is not whether it will be strong enough but whether it will be stiff enough. To put this another way, with modern materials a boat that is adequately stiff is certain to be adequately strong for all normal purposes. The costs of high-performance materials has fallen in recent years and thanks to the aerospace and racing car industries a great deal more is now known about how to use them for best results. Thanks to the FISA minimum weight rules, structural failures are now very rare and the prospective purchaser can turn attention to other considerations, such as impact resistance, longevity, ease of maintenance, and so on.

The hulls of modern boats can be made from a range of materials offering the required combination of strength and stiffness. It is possible to make very light, strong and stiff wooden boats that will perform as well as any made with synthetic materials. Wood has its problems, however. It must be given a tough impervious coating, to keep out moisture and to give the required smooth surface, and this coating may help to overcome the other problem of a soft and easily damaged surface. Such finishes add to the weight but can also add to the strength, especially if they impregnate the wood and help bind the fibres. Wood does tend to creep and some light boats quickly lose their stiffness and shape. Wood is also weak across the grain and tends to split on impact; but this can be alleviated by reinforcement with a synthetic cloth or by laminating to form plywood with alternating grain angles. Unless very thin veneers are used, perhaps laminated on a male mould piece by piece (cold moulding), wood can be reluctant to conform to the shapes demanded by modern hull designs. Good wooden boats require high standards of craftsmanship and are expensive because of this labour-intensive requirement rather than because of the material cost.

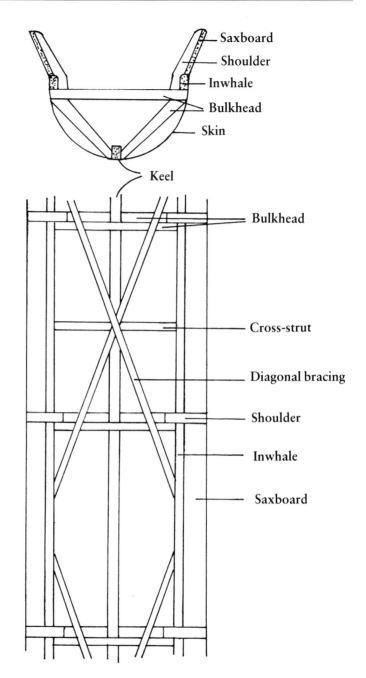

Fig. 62 Traditional wooden
frame construction

SECTION

— Saxboard
— Shoulder
— Inwhale
— Bulkhead
— Skin

— Keel

PLAN

— Bulkhead

— Cross-strut

— Diagonal bracing

— Shoulder

— Inwhale

— Saxboard

Fibre-reinforced plastics (composites), sometimes polyester but more usually the tougher, more adhesive but more expensive epoxy resins, have been used in boatbuilding for many years. Plastics reinforced with high-quality glass fabric (to about 50% of their mass) are quite cheap and have reasonable mechanical properties. They are rather too dense and flexible, so it is common for high-performance boats to be made with the superior but more expensive fabrics such as Kevlar and carbon fibre. The great advantage with most fibre-reinforced plastics is that they are very easy to form into complex shapes whilst the resin is still liquid. In addition it is possible to achieve excellent surface finishes easily by using a highly polished female mould.

Perhaps surprisingly, fibre-reinforced plastic is not impervious to water and tends to absorb it along the fibres. In the long term this water will not only increase weight but may cause the layers to separate (delamination). The solution is to protect the outer surface with a thin layer of tough resin called the gel coat, which also gives damage protection and a good finish. It is therefore most important to look after the surface and to repair damage as soon as possible.

One disadvantage of the synthetic materials is that although they are not susceptible to rot they can be adversely affected by other environmental factors. Both polyester and epoxy resins deteriorate and crack under solar ultraviolet radiation, and these hairline cracks slowly spread. Temperature also affects plastics, and the mixture of materials can cause distortion if boats become too hot. There have been many instances of plastic boats softening in the heat and suffering subsequent delamination or distortion. Manufacturers can use more stable resin systems, especially the thermosetting ones that are baked in an oven to cure them. It is best to keep any boat out of the sun as much as possible, and light colours may be better.

Sandwich composites, where two thin skins are separated by a lightweight honeycomb or foam core, are excellent ways of achieving stiffness with minimum weight and are particularly suited to unitary or monocoque construction (that is, without separate reinforcing struts). This method of construction has the beauty of simplicity and because of it offers the prospect of minimum use of material and least laborious assembly. If only we could all agree on a standard design of boat, or if FISA imposes one, it ought to be possible to mass-produce unitary construction plastic boats of very high performance at much reduced cost. Racing boats are really much too expensive already and most purchasers are buying refinements that are of minimal use for their restricted talents. Of course competitors always want something that is different, and hopefully better; the manufacturers are also competing for customers and it is very much in their interest to continue to offer something special. Perhaps we should also heed the example of other sports where the imposition of 'one design' has led to a very costly search for tiny advantages just within the rules.

BOAT ERGONOMICS

In order to work at maximum efficiency the athlete must be placed in the boat in the optimum way. The relationship of the athlete's feet, seat and hands to the structure of the boat, the waterline and the oar or sculls are all very important. To some extent this depends on the latest ideas on technique or rig, but it also depends on the dimensions and weight of the athletes in the boat. To some extent the variations can be accommodated by adjustable fittings but the boatbuilder will also have to depart from the ideal structure in order to meet those needs. For example, a higher deck in the centre of the boat will help to stiffen the structure, but the height of the deck determines sitting height, and there is an optimum (rather low) position for that relative to the water line. Quite small differences in such dimensions have effects not only on performance but also on how comfortable and confident the athlete feels in the boat.

Fig. 63 shows the layout of these crucial parts of the 'stateroom' and gives some typical dimensions which long experience has shown to be of the right order. Many of these dimensions are adjustable and guidelines as to how the adjustments should be made and how they effect performance follow later in the chapter.

OARS AND SCULLS

Essentially, oars and sculls are drag devices; they produce thrust primarily by slipping reluctantly through the water and causing the water to react against the blade. However, the slippage represents an efficiency loss because the blade is acting as a fulcrum against which we lever the boat through the water – if the fulcrum slips backwards then the boat does not move so far forwards. Increasing the blade area can reduce slippage but there are practical, technical and even aerodynamic constraints on the maximum size. Even with the biggest blades it is unlikely that the efficiency of an oar (useful power output in relation to human power input) will exceed 75% – the rest of our energy goes into disturbing the air and water.

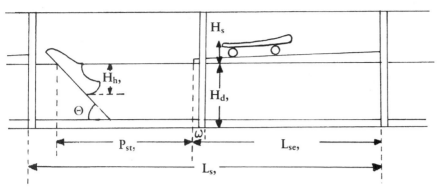

Fig. 63 Dimensions of the rowing 'stateroom', side view

L_s	= Length of stateroom	1,400 mm
L_{se}	= Length of slidetrack (position often adjustable)	720–800 m
W	= work through (past pin) (commonly adjustable)	0–100 mm
H_d	= Height of deck	Very variable but relates to: 1 Height of deck above waterline, 0–15 mm 2 Height of swivel above seat, 150–170 mm
P_{st}	= Position of stretcher	Fully adjustable
H_h	= Height of heels	150 ± 50 mm (usually adjustable)
Θ	= stretcher angle	40–45° (often adjustable)
H_s	= Height of seat	65 ± 5 mm

The motion of an oar through the water, when it is attached to a boat moving in one direction while its blade slips in the other, is complex (fig. 64). We can see that the oar is pivoting about a point some way inboard from the tip of the blade, and this effect can be observed from above, especially if we have some object nearby in the water as a point of reference. For rowing this turning point is about 50–60 cm from the tip, and rather less for a sculling blade, but the exact figures depend on the area and length of the blade and just how far it is slipping. The significance of this is that any part of the oar or scull inboard of that point will be moving in the same direction as the boat, so if it is in the water it will create unnecessary drag retarding the boat rather than propelling it. Good technique just covers the blade and no more. Karl Adam developed blades that were 60 cm long and 20 cm wide to fit these criteria, and they were so successful at the championships in Macon that they have been called 'Macon' blades ever since.

Fig. 64 Movements of the oar
during the stroke. Note that
with the catch at 35° the initial
movement of the blade is in
the same direction as the boat
is moving. The blade effectively
rotates about a point some
way inboard

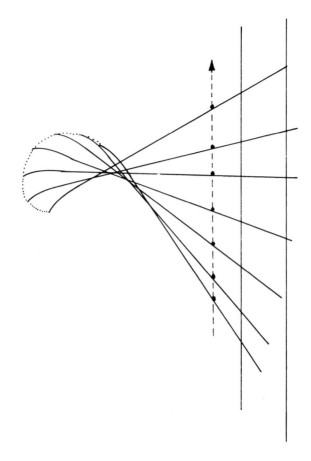

Fig. 65 Macon and big blade

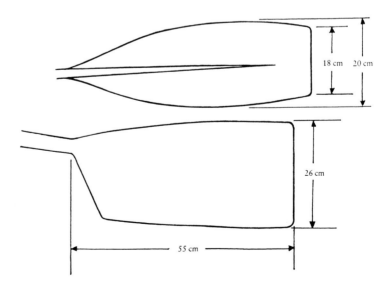

Simply increasing the width of the blades is a mixed blessing because if the bigger blade slips less, then it should be shorter – which would reduce the area again! The wider blade would also have to be buried deeper to cover the top edge. The 'Big Blades' or 'Cleavers', from Concept and other makers, get round these problems through a combination of features; the blades are wide and short to give extra area and allowance for the new turning point; they are asymmetric so that the major part of the blade is below the centre of the loom, and they have a narrow neck at the turning point (fig. 65). These blades are also angled so that as the blade approaches or leaves the water its lowest edge is nearly parallel with the water surface to give cleaner entry or exit. This latter point can be particularly significant with shorter sculls used with a high rig where they will be at a considerable angle from your hands down to the water.

Since flow of water off the face of the blade during its peculiar motion through the water represents lost efficiency, the curvature of the blade also helps to grip the water and create more drag and thrust. Excessive curvature is counterproductive and leads to messy finishes, and it is usual for sculling blades, which sweep through greater arcs, to be flatter than rowing blades. It has been suggested that the curved shape of the blade generates some useful lift as the water flows over it and that this would reduce slippage. If we look again at fig. 64 we can see that when the blade enters the water it is at an acute angle to the boat, and then initially moves outward such that the water flow is along the blade from tip to neck. This could cause pressure differences between the two sides of the curved blade. Scullers reach through even more acute angles, sliding the blade in almost lengthwise to good effect, ensuring solid contact with the water. Be that as it may, it is tempting to believe that deeply dished or odd shaped blades may offer some advantage but in practice little can be gained. At the time of writing it is noticeable that many top crews have reverted to the original 'Big Blade' after experiments with other shapes.

Commonly accepted oar lengths changed little in the hundred years after the invention of the outrigger, but bigger and more compact blades with less slip, and a centre of pressure further outboard, mean that the overall length must be reduced to keep the effective gearing the same. The section on rig, which follows, explains how to choose the appropriate dimensions and how to make best use of the adjustments provided on modern oars and sculls. Carbon fibre reinforced plastic blades and looms offer considerable weight savings over the older wooden ones – the weight saving could be worth more than a quarter-length advantage to an eight over 2,000 metres. The lighter oar also

Fig. 66 The strain in the loom of the oars is apparent as maximum power is applied soon after the start

saves energy as it is moved about and rotated each stroke. The oar must be torsionally stiff so that the blade maintains its proper angle in the water, and it must not bend too much or energy that should be propelling the boat will be lost. On the other hand a very stiff shaft feels harsh and is rather tricky to handle; so most makers offer a range of reasonable stiffness. It should be borne in mind that the feel of an oar or scull also depends on its point of balance outboard.

Research has shown that the most efficient diameter for a handle is about that of the usual sculling grip, which implies that most rowing handles are too thick. Certainly if made of wood (which some athletes prefer) they do need to be thicker than composite ones in order to be strong enough, but still ought to be of a size that fits nicely in the curved fingers. Too fat a handle is harder to pull on, encourages tension and can lead to cramp and clumsy bladework. Beware of new handles, or materials you are not used to, they are very likely to cause blisters (see figs 22 and 24).

RIGGING AND ADJUSTMENTS

The purpose of individually adjustable boats, riggers and oars or sculls is twofold. First of all to ensure that you are in the best possible relationship to your equipment, and secondly so that you can maintain the optimum length of stroke, rating and rhythm.

Position in the boat

As explained earlier, the position of the stretcher, and to a lesser extent the height of your feet on it, determines your position in the boat, but the most significant point of reference is your position relative to the rigger pin(s). This determines the angles you can reach at the catch and finish. For a first approximation, it is usual to place the stretcher so that with the legs fully extended the aft edge of the seat will be 46–48 cm from a line through the pin(s). This will give something like the correct angle at the finish, and can then be more carefully adjusted to give the exact arc that suits best (see table 2). If your legs are particularly long or short you will need to set the stretcher further away or nearer to you and you may need to alter the rig, as explained later, to enable you to row through the desired arc. Checks can be carried out by marking the saxboards with coloured tape, or by attaching vertical straws, to show where the oars or sculls should be at catch and finish. I find it particularly useful to watch crews from above passing underneath a bridge to see what everyone is doing.

Table 2 shows the total arcs and angles of catch and finish being used by top internationals using rigs within the range that is commonly accepted.

Table 2 Measured arcs and angles for rowing and sculling

	Total stroke arc (degrees)	Angles to boat (degrees, catch–finish)
Men rowing	85–93	35–125
Women rowing	80–85	45–125
Men sculling	107–112	30–137
Women sculling	100–106	37–137

The height of the feet can be adjusted in most boats to enable you to achieve comfortably the desired compromise between body swing and leg compression with the best joint angles – as was explained from a biomechanical point of view in Chapter 3. If you have long legs or stiff ankles then you may find it helpful to lower the feet. There is sometimes a problem with long slides rubbing on the backs of the calves, and raising the feet a little may help with this. It is worth experimenting on the ergo with different foot heights where you can measure objectively what difference it makes, and try different leg and body angles as well – people differ, and it is important to find what gives you the best results. Stretcher angles are usually about 42–45 degrees and are adjustable in some boats, but in fact the adjustment is so rarely used that it is often done away with for simplicity and weight saving. If it is adjustable it is often wrong and nobody has thought to correct it!

The height of the swivel above the seat is important in dictating the direction in which you pull the handles and also affects the likely depth of the blade in the water. If the height is too great the blade is more likely to wash out at the finish, and if too low the blade may go too deep. A low rigger also makes it more difficult to extract the blade at the finish and may cause you to lean away from the rigger in an attempt to compensate. The height is measured by placing a straight edge across the boat on top of the saxboards, then measuring down to the lowest part of the seat and up to the middle of the sill of the swivel. More sophisticated rigging sticks are available for the same purpose. A height of about 16–18 cm is a good starting point for most boats, though some scullers prefer considerably more (for example, one recent junior champion sculled on 24 cm), and remember that the left-hand sculling swivel is often 1 cm higher than the other.

It is worth checking that the two saxboards are in fact level – in older boats in particular they may not be. The other problem is that the boat may be twisted, so that although all the rigger heights are set correctly in relation to their seats, the riggers will be at different heights from the water. This problem is not uncommon because boats may twist with time, especially if they are racked badly, but it also happens with some new plastic boats if they are not fully cured by the time they are taken out of their moulds. The twist can be seen if you put a straight edge across the saxboards at both ends of the boat and then sight along from one end, or check with a spirit level. A slight twist can be compensated for with the usual adjustments to height, but a more severe twist requires drastic remedial action by the maker.

Fig. 67 A straight edge across the saxboards will enable the height of the swivel to be checked in relation to the seat. Two such sticks will show any twist in the hull

Gearing

The oar is a lever which pivots round the blade in the water when you pull on the handle, and it pushes the boat along at the point where the loom bears on the pin – though from your point of view when sitting in the boat it may seem that the oar pivots round the pin and levers the water past the boat. Geometrically it does not matter which way you look at it, but I think it is preferable to have a mental image of a fixed blade as being more efficient than hurling water sternwards. The overall length of the oar or scull and the position of the button will therefore determine how far the boat moves for each stroke you take. This is what we mean by gearing, but it is a bit more complicated than say the gearing on a bicycle because the bike crank always goes through 360 degrees, but we sweep through a range of total arcs from catch to finish. The angular length of the stroke depends on four major interacting factors:

1   The inboard length from the button to end of the handle.
2   The distance of the rigger pin from the centre line of the boat (the thwartship distance or TD).
3   Your height and arm spread.
4   Your range of movement, which in turn depends on your flexibility and style of rowing or sculling.

As explained earlier, the amount of blade slip also affects how far the boat moves per stroke, so changes in blade size or shape may need to be accompanied by changes in gearing.

These gearing dimensions are of great importance in determining how quickly you can move the handle and how hard it feels, and are thus crucial to your ability to maintain your desired rating and rhythm in the prevailing conditions.

Experience shows that for each boat type there is a small range of settings for the TD and inboard length that will give good results for most athletes (assuming a standard overall length of oar or scull). Too light a gearing and you will not be able to move fast enough to reach maximum speed or the rushed effort to do so will be too tiring. If the gearing is too severe the work will be too hard and you will tire more rapidly or be unable to maintain a high enough rating. For any given oar or scull length, light gearing means more inboard and perhaps also a greater TD, whilst the most severe gearing will come from a combination of short inboard and short TD. For adverse conditions such as a headwind it is usual to leave the TD alone and extend the inboard by 1 cm or so. For tailwinds a higher gearing is worth trying so that ratings are not too great.

If the purpose of rigging adjustments is to ensure that the crew or sculler can cover the course at an optimum rating and rhythm, then it is probably true that the commonest mistake is 'overgearing'. This is usually because of an ill founded optimism about strength or stamina, or in the macho belief that that bigger oars or more severe gearing will necessarily make the boat go faster. If a crew or sculler is already at the limit, then a rig that imposes even a half stroke a minute drop in rating can lose 1–2 seconds over a 2,000-metre course, even though the blade is moving further each stroke.

There is a common fallacy that changes in the TD alone will have a large and simple effect on gearing (e.g. 'changing the TD by 1 cm is equivalent to moving the button by 3 cm'). On their own they may not, but they may have a significant effect on the biomechanics of the stroke which will change the arc. It is true, however, that the relationship of TD and inboard length is critical and has a profound effect on the length of stroke and gearing (fig. 68), so these are the figures that you must get right.

Irrespective of these other considerations there is one other parameter that has become well established. This is the value called 'overlap' (fig. 69). In rowing this is the amount by which the inboard (measured from the outer face of the button to the end of the handle) exceeds the TD, and it is almost universally set at 30–31 cm. Values very far from this will place the

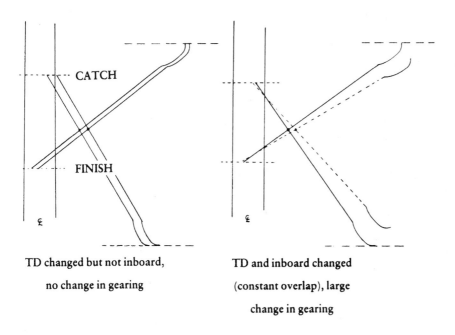

Fig. 68 Effects of changes in TD and inboard length

TD changed but not inboard, no change in gearing

TD and inboard changed (constant overlap), large change in gearing

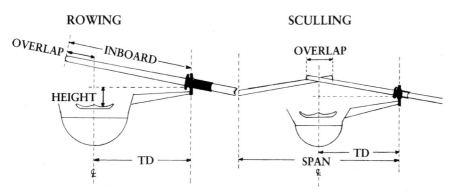

Fig. 69 Overlap in rowing and sculling

outside hand in an awkward position, and can lead to a number of other technical problems such as leaning away from the rigger at the finish.

In sculling, the overlap can be defined in the same way, though it is more commonly expressed as the actual overlap of the two handles. A value of about 8 cm (depending on individual needs) would be usual when measured in the first way, and this should give a true overlap of 16 cm. This does not allow for the extra distance between the button face and the centre of the pin (from where the TD is measured) caused by the width of the swivel. In reality, therefore, the actual overlap of the two handles will be about 19–20 cm (and in rowing perhaps we should add 2 cm for the same reason). You will be glad to know that

Fig. 70 Overlap in a sculling boat can be measured in a number of different ways – be careful when reading rigging charts!

these details are usually safely ignored and rigging tables (such as the ones in this book) take the TD from the centre of the pin, and the inboard from the button face, and disregard the difference.

The rigging tables that follow (table 3) illustrate current practice. The great danger is to apply them too slavishly – they are guidelines only.

Table 3 Suggested rigs

TD is given from the centre of the pin, and for sculling boats the total spread or span from one pin to the other is used. All dimensions are in cm.

	Overall (Macon blade)	Overall (Big blade)	Inboard	TD or span
Men				
1X	298–300	290–292	88–9	160–62
2X	298–300	290–292	88	160
4X	298–300	290–292	88	159
2+	383–385	375–378	117	87
2–	383–385	375–378	116.5	86.5
4+	383–385	375–378	115.5	85.5
4–	383–385	375–378	115	85
8+	383–385	375–378	114	84.5

(Lightweight men will use overall lengths at the lower end of the range given)

	Overall (Macon blade)	Overall (Big blade)	Inboard	TD or span
Women				
1X	298	289–291	88	160
2X	298	289–291	88	159
4X	298	289–291	87.5	158.5
2–	380–382	372–375	116.5	86
4+	380–382	372–375	116	85.5
4–	380–382	372–375	115.5	85
8+	380–382	372–375	114.5	84.5

(Lightweight women will use overall lengths at the lower end of the range given)

	Overall (Macon blade)	Overall (Big blade)	Inboard	TD or span
Junior 1X				
age 17–18	298	288	87–88	159
15–16	296	285	86–87	158
13–14	294	282	85–86	157
9–12	285	–	83–84	156

These figures are based on the rigs used by a number of the most successful teams in recent years, and they are typical of the dimensions employed by the characteristically tall and powerful athletes of the best crews. For those shorter in stature, the principle is that in order to retain the overlap and desired angles of the blade at catch and finish, the inboard and TD should both be reduced by about 1 cm, whilst the overall length needs to be shorter by about 3 cm to retain the appropriate gearing.

Rigging for smaller people and slower boats

Amongst single scullers it has long been accepted that their own boat and sculls should be adjusted to their body size, and the principle has always been that the smaller sculler has shorter sculls overall, with a reduced rigger span and inboard on the sculls. In this way it can be arranged that all scullers sweep their sculls through much the same angles but without imposing excessively hard or light gearing. Boys or girls who are exceptionally tall for their age would use a wider span and a greater inboard, but their lesser strength means that they should use a shorter scull overall than their older peers.

The same principles can apply equally well to crew rowing, but in practice a rather different philosophy has grown up that we should adjust the rig according to the boat type and its expected speed rather than to the individuals in it. Now that adjustable length oars are freely available we could individualize each crewmember's rig – but there are pragmatic reasons against this, especially if equipment is shared, and it is rarely done except for extremely tall or short people in a fixed crew.

It is common to use wider TD with longer inboard as a way of easing the gearing for smaller and slower crews, not just slower boat types. I think that this is not the best approach and my experience suggests that the 'body size approach' may be better. I believe that we should be giving such crews shorter oars, with *less* inboard and *narrower* rigger spreads, so that they can move them through more nearly the same angles as their bigger brethren do, but not be over-geared. Another approach would be to reduce blade size to induce more slip, but this is inherently less efficient.

I'm afraid that there doesn't seem to be any easy or universal formula that will give the answers, for there are too many variables. So the best we can do is apply the principles and then test for the best compromise.

Angles on the pin, swivel face and blade

Because the pull on the handle is slightly upwards (5–10 degrees was suggested earlier), there will be a tendency for the blade to be driven too deep in the water. A positive pitch (angle to the vertical) counter-acts this tendency so the top of the blade is tilted a little towards the stern. The exact angle required depends on the height of the swivel in relation to the athlete, and the individual's technique. For both rowing and sculling, experienced athletes would commonly use 4–6 degrees of stern pitch, and although novices might at first be happier with more they should soon learn to use the lesser amount. If large amounts of stern pitch are required then there is something wrong – it may be poor technique or it may be a twisted blade or a bent rigger. Excessive pitch will tend to cause the blade to lose its grip on the water and wash out, whereas under-pitching is likely to make the blade go too deep.

There is a natural tendency to pull upwards more at the beginning of the stroke, and then downwards at the finish as the arms bend (which is why slide beds usually incline upwards towards back stops). Thus there is a need for more pitch at the catch and less at the finish. This can be achieved by leaning the pin outwards a degree or two, and this is called lateral pitch to distinguish it from the stern pitch described above. It can either be built into the rigger, or there may be a separate adjustment for it. At the catch some of this lateral pitch will be added to the stern pitch of the swivel face and any angle built into the blade, so giving more total pitch. At the finish the lateral pitch will subtract slightly from the total. This relationship holds good as long as the pin is vertical in the fore and aft plane, but inclining the pin fore or aft to achieve changes in stern pitch can have unfortunate effects on the way in which total pitch changes through the stroke. It is much better to make adjustments with a variable-pitch swivel and leave the pin alone.

The usual standard is to put the 4–6 degrees into the face of the swivel, and have either 2 or 0 degrees built into the oar or scull. 1–2 degrees of lateral pitch then gives a range through the stroke that should suit most athletes. In my view it would be wise to ensure that all oars and sculls in a club are zero pitched so that there is never any problem when they are used in different boats, and then all adjustments and measurements are made on the boats as necessary. The effects of variations on these figures are shown in table 4.

Table 4 Effect on blade pitch of pin angle

Pin angle°		Pitch on blade°		
Lateral	Stern	Catch	Middle	Finish
Swivel face 4°, oar 0°				
2	0	5.2	4.0	3.2
2	1	5.6	5.0	3.8
2	2	6.0	6.0	4.4
1	0	4.6	4.0	3.6
1	1	5.0	5.0	4.2
1	2	5.4	6.0	4.8
0	0	4.0	4.0	4.0
0	1	4.4	5.0	4.6
0	2	4.8	6.0	5.2
Swivel face 4°, oar 2° (NB: This is the same as 6° on the swivel face, alone)				
2	0	7.2	6.0	5.2
2	1	7.6	7.0	5.8
2	2	8.4	8.0	6.4
1	0	6.6	6.0	5.6
1	1	7.0	7.0	6.2
1	2	7.4	8.0	6.8
0	0	6.0	6.0	6.0
0	1	6.4	7.0	6.6
0	2	6.8	8.0	7.2

Unfortunately riggers are easily disturbed by bumps or scrapes, and not all pitch-adjusting devices are reliable, so it is wise to check regularly, but most importantly when a boat has just been re-assembled or before a race. Wooden oars in particular can vary quite a lot in pitch, even within a set, and may change with time, so do check them as well.

Rigging a boat

If you are checking or resetting the rig on a boat it is always best to be methodical and not to assume things that you have not checked. The boat should be firmly supported right way up on trestles and if at all possible should be level both fore and aft and across (check with a spirit level). Although modern pitch gauges allow you to compensate it is much easier if the boat is level, and you are less likely to make mistakes. Prop the boat so that it cannot move. If the riggers have top-stays then take off the top nut or bolt and lift them off – this is because a maladjusted stay can distort the whole rigger and it may have to come off anyway for some adjustments. Check that the other rigger bolts are tight, and do make sure that the riggers are in the right place! Check the TD first, using a rigging stick to ensure that you are measuring horizontally, by measuring the width of the boat, halving that figure and then measuring from the saxboard to the centre of the pin (fig. 71). When the TD is right, mark it so that you can see at a glance

Fig. 71 Measuring the TD

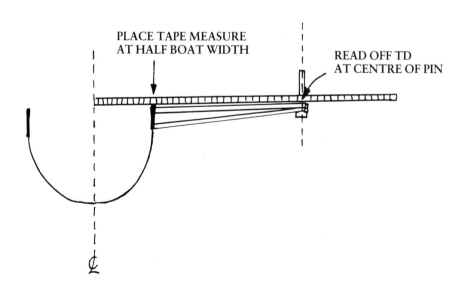

PLACE TAPE MEASURE
AT HALF BOAT WIDTH

READ OFF TD
AT CENTRE OF PIN

Fig. 72 Using a pitch gauge to measure stern pitch. In this case the spirit level must first be set on a horizontal part of the boat

in future whether it has altered. Now use the rigging stick to determine the swivel height above the lowest part of the seat (fig. 67).

It is arguable that the pitch should be measured on the blade itself since this is the bit going in the water, but it is not easy to do accurately because the blade is curved and needs to be held at exactly the correct angle to the boat. I prefer to measure the pitches (stern and lateral) on the pins and swivels themselves (fig. 72) and do a separate check on the oars and sculls – I would rather know that all were right. Once the adjustment is secured then adjust the top stay so that it will just drop back into position without any strain, and do up its retaining nut or bolt – they are notorious for coming loose so ensure that they have shake-proof washers or self-locking nuts. Never go out for a race without being certain that your riggers are correctly adjusted and that all bolts are tight. Take a spanner!

6 General Principles of Training

The human body is remarkably adaptable and if properly trained will become capable of physical feats which could only be dreamt of at the outset; what was once difficult becomes easy, and what was impossible comes within reach. The great Czech distance runner Emil Zatopek said that by an effort of the will it was possible to change the whole body. To a considerable extent he was right, but we are also prisoners of our inheritance, so ultimately we cannot do more than improve through training to the limit of our inherited abilities. Recent research has begun to identify some of the genes which determine our ability to respond to various types of training, and some gloomy interpretations suggest that there are those who are unable to respond – but I have never met any in a lifetime of rowing coaching! Fortunately rowing and sculling are very rewarding sports in this respect, for no one, however great their athletic potential, can have any success without training and everyone, however young or old, will improve with training, often to a remarkable extent.

In the earlier chapters on the techniques of both rowing and sculling, I made the point that all training should be regarded as an opportunity to learn and improve skills, even if the prime purpose was to increase fitness or strength. Thus training must have a number of objectives and desired effects, which is only to be expected when the sport requires a unique combination of skill, endurance, strength and speed. The principal objectives of training then should be to improve in all the following aspects of performance:

1 *Skill*

It is useless to be strong and fit but unable to row or scull efficiently. Of course the beginner needs to devote most time and effort to the development of this quality and will gain most from it, but even the most experienced athlete can refine skills still further. To row or scull well requires at least adequate strength in all the muscles used, and to keep on doing it demands endurance – so skill training cannot be divorced from the other aspects of training. Looking at it the other way, poor co-ordination will reduce effective strength, and poor technique will reduce endurance.

Learning new skills or reinforcing old ones is best done when the body is free from fatigue, but on the other hand the maintenance of technique under stress is vital in competition, so that too must be rehearsed. As in many other sports it is possible to reach a stage where despite continued training there is no further measurable improvement in physical fitness, and yet race performance does get better still. This effect is most likely to be due to further improvements in skill; that is, the efficiency with which the muscles are used to propel the boat (including tactics and pace judgement), and also in the realms of psychology.

2 *Endurance*

Rowing and sculling events are certainly biased towards endurance, for even the so-called sprint events are at least 500 metres and require very hard work for anything up to two minutes, whilst the standard regatta distance of 2,000 metres requires considerable stamina. The need for endurance was recognized a long while ago and the longer-distance Head races of autumn and spring were introduced largely to help promote desirable endurance training, but have now become an important part of the competition scene in their own right. The objective of most of us is to get there first, not just to arrive, and the ability to row a long way slowly does not by itself win races. What is needed is a combination of endurance with speed and with strength - 'general endurance' has a part to play but the athlete needs training that will also develop 'speed endurance' (the ability to maintain speed of movement for a long time), and 'strength endurance' (overcoming a significant resistance repeatedly).

3 *Strength*

Because its mass is being supported by the water, a boat and its occupants can be moved very easily at low speed, but the resistance increases very rapidly as the speed goes up (the power required increases roughly as the cube of the speed). To go that little bit faster than the opposition when you and they are already near to maximum means that much greater force must be exerted. To reach the desired speed demands strength enough to overcome the rapidly rising resistance, but more than that there must be something in reserve – otherwise the effort cannot be sustained. Sheer maximal strength of the type shown by weightlifters is not what we want, but rather the 'strength endurance' referred to above, and, since at speed the movements must also be very rapid, almost explosive, so the athlete must combine strength with speed. Fig. 73 shows diagrammatically how the different components contribute in rowing as compared with some other sports. It is clear from this diagram that endurance is the major component in 2,000m rowing.

Fig. 73 Relationship between speed, strength and endurance for various sports (after Ikai)

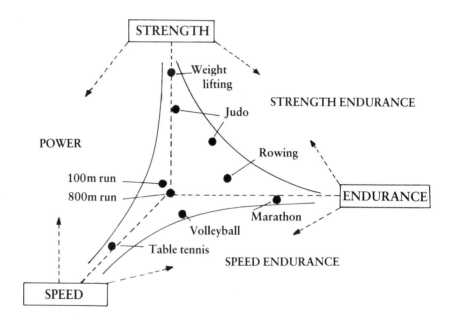

4 *Mobility and flexibility*
Rowing and sculling require the ability to work efficiently through a very large range of movement (fig. 74). If you are inflexible it will make the effort seem harder, will reduce the length of your stroke and may reduce your skill. It has also been increasingly appreciated in recent years that the postural muscles of the trunk (the ones involved in what is called 'core stability') are very important in enabling the whole body to work optimally through the stroke. These core muscles will be helped by specific conditioning exercises, and they can also help in injury prevention by maintaining good posture through the range of movement.

Fig. 74 One of the components of fitness for rowing is flexibility and the ability to work effectively through a large range of movement

5 Psychology

The beginner needs to learn how to train, and it often takes a long time to appreciate just how much hard work is both possible and necessary if success is to be enjoyed. Some training is enjoyable or rewarding in its own right, but much of it is frankly a means to an end, and that end may be very elusive! To make the most of the opportunities you must develop your qualities of determination and persistence, and one of the objectives of a progressive training scheme must be to help that development. This is a tough sport and high levels of performance are actually painful, so mental toughness is essential – but it can be trained like the rest of your body. Young athletes in particular will need to learn that effort is rewarded, that greater or more prolonged efforts bring greater rewards, and that some sacrifices may be worth making.

One of the effects of training is to change the perception of effort so that a given level of performance seems easier, and at the same time tolerance to fatigue will also be improved. Some of these effects are due to adaptations in the body systems, but much is also a reflection of the athlete's psychological make-up and the way that it is modified by experience of training and competition. It is known that brain chemistry is significantly changed by exercise as 'natural opiates' are released within it during stressful effort. These brain chemicals reduce the sensation of pain and are anti-depressant, and we can become so used to the more pleasurable sensations that result that we become almost addicted to exercise!

Young athletes respond to training and racing rather differently to adults. Enjoyment is very important, and although their endurance and strength is far from developed many can be very vigorous. Young children have a much lower perception of effort than teenagers, who in turn would rate an equivalent effort as less demanding than would an adult, and the children also recover much more quickly (at least from short, intense efforts). It is not clear why this should be so – it may be that like all young animals children are naturally much more active in play and games, or it may be that they are in some way less able to stress their bodies.

WHAT HAPPENS IN OUR BODIES WHEN WE TRAIN

When we work hard to move a boat or perform some land training exercises a large number of changes occur in our bodies in order to meet the increased demand for energy and to dispose of the extra waste products and heat. Many of these changes will be temporary, but if the effort exceeds that which we are used to for long enough then the body cells and systems will be stimulated to adapt and change more permanently to meet the challenge. It is important to appreciate that the exercise is stimulating the release of a flood of chemical messengers which have a large range of physiological and even genetic effects, many of which will not occur until the exercise is over. As a result the body will be better equipped next time, which in turn means that the same task will be achieved more easily, so if further improvement is required then the effort should be increased once more. The way in which the body adapts is rather specific to the demand that was placed upon it – thus we have four fundamentals in training which must be followed if the training is to be effective:

1 *Overload*   The effort required must be significant in relation to your present capacity or your body will not be stimulated enough to adapt. This does not mean that we have to believe slogans such as 'no gain without strain', or 'if it doesn't hurt it can't be doing you good', which are not true and might actually be harmful. On the other hand we must not kid ourselves that we can produce exceptional performances unless we have made the necessary effort in training.

2 *Progression*   If continued improvement is to be made then it will be necessary to progressively increase the load in training in response to your increasing capacity. Adaptation happens gradually, though more rapidly at first, and depending on the rate of adaptation, there might be noticeable progression from week to week at one end of the scale and certainly from year to year at the other. Since many of the adaptations are forms of growth, we would expect young athletes to make the most rapid progress. As the body adapts so the priorities in training can also change, for example, from the long-term development of strength and endurance towards more emphasis on speed as the competition period approaches.

3 *Specificity*   To a considerable extent what you get out of your training depends on what you put into it, that is, the body responds in a specific way to a particular type of training. For example, training in a series of short, high-speed bursts with lots of rest in between will develop speed and strength but have little effect on endurance. There is an enormous variety of possible effective training methods, varying in the type of work, its duration, its speed, the strength demanded, the number of times it is repeated and the length of the rest periods – and so on. These possible training methods can be grouped according to their probable specific effects and then a selection made according to the athlete's needs. In practice since a combination of abilities is required the answer is likely to be mixed training, in proportions and at times chosen to bring the best results.

4 *Rest*   Without adequate rest the body does not have time to adapt and instead of progress you will encounter increasing fatigue and failure to adapt. Some forms of training actually cause temporary tissue damage, to which the tissues respond, given time, by not just repairing themselves but growing stronger. Damage them again too soon, however, and not surprisingly they will get worse, not better. Proper

sleep is particularly important because it is only during the deeper phases of sleep that larger amounts of growth hormone are released, and this hormone is essential for the adaptations we are working for.

One of the most important differences in the way our bodies respond to different types of training lies in the different energy production systems that can be used. The anaerobic systems produce extra energy quickly without consuming oxygen and they are particularly essential for the fast starts and finishes required in a regatta. The aerobic system uses oxygen to produce the endurance that we have already seen is our primary need. Fig. 75 illustrates the contribution that these systems make during a 2,000-metre race.

Fig. 75 Aerobic and anaerobic energy supplies during a race

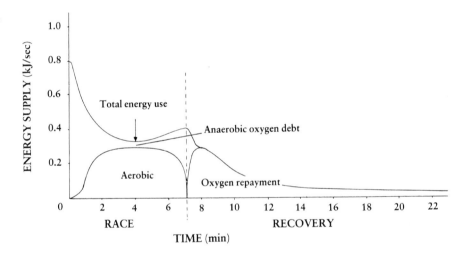

Anaerobic system I does not use oxygen but relies on stored energy in the muscles. These stores only last a few seconds at maximum effort but they are briefly important at the start and finish of a race.

Anaerobic system II also works without oxygen and enables high levels of power to be maintained at the start when that from other sources is not yet adequate, and it can be called upon for extra power in the final sprint. Unfortunately it produces lactic acid as a waste product and if this accumulates it will cause great and painful fatigue, so we cannot use it extensively for very long. The extra oxygen that we will have to take in after the race in order to dispose of the waste products is known as the *oxygen debt*.

Aerobic respiration using oxygen is the most efficient way of producing energy for our muscles and this must cover the bulk of our energy needs in all but the shortest of efforts. Moreover, the greater our capacity for aerobic work the less we have to call upon the fatiguing and short-duration anaerobic systems.

We vary in our inherited potential to use these systems but appropriate training will make an enormous difference to our capacities. The specificity of training applies very much to the way in which we develop. Short, intense efforts will favour the anaerobic systems, while more prolonged training at lower speed will encourage the aerobic side not just in the muscles but in the equally important provision of oxygen to them via the lungs and circulatory system. Since aerobic endurance takes longer to develop, this means that the major part of training must be directed that way.

Finally, the concept of specificity also applies to you as an individual; each of us responds to stress in a different way, so the training programme should be tailored to the individual – but that is less than easy in crew rowing!

THE YOUNG ATHLETE

A very large proportion of competitors enter the sport in their teens or even earlier when skill learning can be most rapid and effective, and when attitudes and habits that will stand them in good stead for the rest of their careers can best be established. Before puberty, skills such as balance in a single scull can be learnt very quickly, and it would be a waste of opportunity not to move on to such more challenging craft. Physically, though, the pre-pubescent child responds rather differently to training than does the teenager or adult. Research shows that aerobic training for the youngest age groups has most to commend it, for the low-intensity exercise will have many benefits for the development and maintenance of a good circulatory and respiratory system and will have a general stimulatory effect on growth. Anaerobic training does not seem to have the same effect as in adults and in any case very intense training with heavy loads cannot be recommended for children who have incomplete reinforcement of the skeleton and other supporting tissues. Since this sport involves overcoming resistance the strength and effectiveness of the muscles will increase, but we cannot expect much muscular growth until the hormonal changes of puberty have occurred. Children are easily bored and the challenge for the coach is to devise very varied and fun ways for the youngsters to enjoy learning new skills and gaining all-round development.

After puberty, training can be progressively increased and progress is likely to be very rapid in all respects as growth and maturity advance, although in some cases the growth is so rapid that temporary problems of poor co-ordination may intrude. Weight training will be beneficial to muscular development now, but care must be taken not to damage the developing skeleton with very heavy loads. In my experience the risks of heavy weight training need to be very carefully considered and I am not convinced that its benefits outweigh other methods of strength development with this age group. The evidence is that the emphasis still needs to be on aerobic training and that too much anaerobic work could be harmful to the developing systems, or at least unproductive in the longer term. It was for this reason that the standard racing distance for juniors was increased to 2,000 metres, and events such as the Schools' Head were lengthened.

Fig. 76 Parents, teachers and supporters value the participation of young athletes in our sport

At this age parents and teachers often become concerned about the time and effort being expended on rowing. I firmly believe that the benefits to physical and mental health are so important that active participation in sport must be positively encouraged, and I do not believe that enough time cannot be found in the day for adequate training, even at very high levels, without harm to academic progress. My own experience over many years matches that of others who have found that well organized participation in rowing is in fact beneficial academically. Other large-scale studies have shown that those who were most successful and active in sport also tended to do better academically and to find the most worthwhile careers. This is not to say that sport must become an obsession, but rather it should be an enhancing part of a full life and deserving of a high priority.

FEMALE ATHLETES

I do not believe that anything in this chapter does not apply equally to both males and females and I think it wrong to assume that a female's ultimate capacities are very different to the male's. Indeed, it is the unfortunate view of the 'weaker sex' that has greatly retarded women's progress in sport. Nevertheless there are differences which should be taken into account in devising training schemes that are tailored to individual requirements.

On average, and one should stress that exceptional competitors are by definition *not* average, women have a smaller proportion of muscle mass, smaller hearts and lungs, and smaller blood volumes and haemoglobin levels than equivalent men. As a result they will have less strength and lower oxygen uptake levels. However, all the evidence suggests that women respond to aerobic training in much the same way as men and with the same beneficial results. The difference between trained and untrained subjects is much greater than the inherent differences between men and women. Because of the typical differences in hormonal patterns most women do not respond to weight training in quite the same way as men and may not increase muscle mass quite so markedly. The characteristic differences in the skeleton (narrower shoulders, wider pelvis) do not seem to be important in our sport, but the fact that women tend to have less upper body strength may be. It could be useful for female competitors to put more emphasis on countering this weakness, particularly in land training.

Are there any special dangers for women? Well, some worry about developing 'unfeminine' muscle bulk, but it seems that women are able to make very substantial strength gains without much increase in muscle mass. The fit female athlete has a lower proportion of body fat than her untrained sister, and thus her muscles may be better defined – but who is to say that a toned body is unattractive? Some women who train very hard find that their menstrual cycles become irregular or may even temporarily cease (amenorrhoea), and this condition must be avoided by girls. Even where this state is maintained for many years it would seem to be easily reversible by a reduction in training, and is not likely to result in any permanent loss in fertility. Many female athletes use the contraceptive pill as a convenient way to control menstruation and thus avoid problems with forthcoming training peaks or competition. There is some concern that prolonged amenorrhoea may lead to loss of bone mineralization, but again this seems to be reversible in young women and may be countered to some extent by dietary supplements. The full explanation is not yet clear and it does not seem to rest on proportions of body fat, as was at one time thought. In other women, and particular in older ones, the evidence is that exercise (more particularly load bearing) is important in maintaining the mass and strength of the skeleton.

METHODS OF TRAINING AND THEIR EFFECTS

In Chapter 7 the physiological and anatomical effects of training are discussed in much more detail, but at this stage the aim is to outline the methods and to summarize their scientific rationale so that effective programmes can be put together according to your needs. Referring again to the concept of specificity, we need to define the intensity, duration and rest intervals for each type of work, for these will determine precisely what effect the training has. In other words, you must look for the *quality* and *quantity* of training that will give you what you want. Research in sports science covers a huge area, only part of which may be applicable to our particular sport, and it brings with it a great deal of jargon – fortunately we don't need to know it all, but we shall have to use some terminology that is well established in rowing.

How to measure quality

The maximum capacity of the body to use oxygen (maximum aerobic work capacity) is expressed as VO_2 max., and it is invaluable to be able to define the intensity of a training session in terms of the percentage of your VO_2 max. that is demanded, or at least some more convenient estimate that is based upon it. What we need is a simple way of translating what is on our training schedule into a personal level of effort that will give us the desired effect.

Training intensities below 50% of VO_2 max. have little effect on improving any form of endurance, whilst very high intensities (above 100%, say) can improve anaerobic capacity but not aerobic endurance. The *anaerobic threshold* or AT is when the demand for energy from the muscles means that a significant extra contribution begins to be made by the anaerobic systems on top of that from the aerobic process. It is also called the *lactate threshold* because the amount of that substance increases measurably in the blood above the amount found at lesser intensities. The threshold varies from person to person and with fitness levels, but will be at about 70% (and perhaps up to 90% in rare cases) of VO_2 max. Runners use words like 'easy', 'steady' or 'hard' to describe levels of continuous effort below AT, but in British rowing at any rate the terms UT1 and UT2 have been adopted for the same purpose. UT stands for *utilization training* and the 1 or 2 denote the different levels of aerobic work, where 2 is the less intense.

It has been shown that the most effective intensity for training aerobic capacity is around the level of AT, but it is also understood that more prolonged efforts at lower intensities (UT1 or UT2) can have more beneficial effects in the long term. The snag is that continuous work at AT or above is difficult even for very experienced athletes and such intensity demands more recovery and rest. Work above the threshold increases lactic acid production rapidly and this in itself will limit the length of the work periods. The solution is to use some form of interrupted, repetition, or interval training – that is, periods of hard work alternating with periods of easier effort or rest. Interrupted training helps prevent excessive lactate build up and allows these higher work levels to be repeated, and in effect enables the body to be trained at higher intensities for longer. Work just above the threshold is described as *transitional* or *transport*, TR, and even higher intensities as *anaerobic*, AN, or *lactate*, L, or even *alactate*, A-LT.

For most of us it is not practicable to measure oxygen uptake directly, but fortunately it is known that there is a close relationship between heart rate and VO_2. Although the figures may differ somewhat from person to person, the heart rate can be used as a practical individual guide to training intensity and is easily measured from the pulse or by using a monitor. These matters are explored more fully in the next chapter. Table 5 gives these approximate heart rate figures and their equivalents.

Table 5 Heart rate and intensity equivalents

Heart rate bpm	% VO$_2$ max.	Effort level
135–155	50–60	UT2, easy/steady
155–165	60–70	UT1, somewhat hard
165–175	70–80	Threshold, AT, hard
175–185	80–90	Transitional, TR, very hard
185–210	90–100	A-LT, maximum

With experience it is possible to relate these measures of training intensity to speed over a certain distance while training, or to boat speed if you have the equipment. Subjective estimates of 'pressure' have traditionally been used and are still valid, as are rates of striking; and personal ratings of effort have also been shown to be quite reliable guides. The Borg Rating of Perceived Exertion scale, RPE (table 6), is a well-accepted way of recording the quality of the work done.

Table 6 Borg Rating of Perceived Exertion scale

Rating	Descriptor	Rowing pressure
0	Rest	
1	Very, very easy	} Light
2	Easy	
3	Moderate	Half pressure
4	Somewhat hard	} Firm
5	Hard	
7	Very hard	Full pressure
10	Maximal	Sprint

Another way of recording the total effort of a session quite objectively is to multiply the work time in minutes by the heart rate, or by the % of maximum heart rate. The figure obtained is referred to as TRIMP (training volume × training intensity or impulse). You can of course combine TRIMP with RPE to obtain a full record and impression of the session.

Quantity

It is tempting to look at the training of the Olympic champions and to think that it must be the ideal for everyone. Well, if you are one of the best athletes in the country and you are determined to win a medal at the next Olympiad then you should, by current standards, become a full-time professional athlete and train six hours a day, seven days a week and for forty-nine weeks of the year. I suspect though that the majority of readers will have a very different question to ask – something like, 'I can manage one or two hours most days, so what should I do to be as good as possible?' Part of the answer to that question is not to expect a watered down version of the Olympian's training to be effective.

Tim Foster described his training for the Sydney Olympics as time on the treadmill, grinding it out day, after day, after day: 20 km on the water early in the morning, an hour in the gym on a weight circuit, and then another 16–20 km on the water or ergometer. Most of this work

Fig. 77 Pinsent and Foster overhaul the DDR crew to win the 1988 Junior World Championships. State support for the Eastern Bloc crews enabled them to devote much time to the pursuit of very high standards

would be at low intensity, and indeed it would have to be because no human could work at 100% all the time without breakdown. The effect of this very prolonged and very tough training is to produce the great physiological changes that make an Olympic medal possible. So why shouldn't we all try the same approach? For one thing, even if we had the time and the determination, most of us would be unable to profit from such a demanding regime. We could not absorb so much work and instead of adapting and progressing we would fail. I know several fine young athletes who have been destroyed by their attempt to follow training schedules that were inappropriate for them.

There is no doubt that it is quite possible to reach a very high standard indeed on much less training, and the secret is finding the intensity and balance of training methods through the year that optimizes the time you have available. If the Olympian must spend a very large proportion of his or her (greater) time at low intensities then it does not follow that you must do the same. A judicious mix of faster paced work with adequate steadier sessions can be very rewarding and can also help to ensure that you do not become an 'endurance stereotype'. We have already seen that work near to the threshold is the most productive of improvement in VO_2 max., at least in the shorter term, and if you are only training once per day then the longer recovery required is partly taken care of. You should not be too concerned that the lesser training hours will not produce adequate levels of endurance – after all the Olympic marathon runners employ fewer training hours than our oarsmen and women.

It is well established that three to five good training sessions per week are enough to bring about very substantial gains, and that further sessions are of diminishing value (though doubtless necessary to give the small advantages that are required for success in intense competition). For the very young athlete three sessions are probably enough, especially for the active youngster who wants to do other things. The ambitious school first eight rower will, like the prospective junior international, be trying to find fourteen hours or so of training time in the week, as will the better club competitor. And if you want to go further than that and you are advanced enough to absorb the training without giving up the day job? Then do what many runners do and get up early to fit in a second session of lower effort (but good enough to have a useful effect), or increase what you do each weekend. Mileage makes champions, but don't neglect the quality as well.

Table 7 summarizes the characteristics and likely effects of the forms of training most commonly used. It is up to you and your coach to

Table 7 Some methods of training and their effects

Rowing, sculling, ergometer, running

Intensity	Durations of work periods	Repetitions	Length of rest	Effect
1 Low <70% VO_2 max. UT2	1hr+	Continuous	0	Long-term aerobic, recovery Basic technique
2 Moderate-high, up to anaerobic threshold UT1	½-2hr, or 10min -½hr	Continuous, or 2-4	0 or 5-10 min	Very good aerobic capacity and endurance
3 Alternate moderate/high (below and above anaerobic threshold UT1/TR	1-8min each, total <2hr	Continuous	0	Very good aerobic capacity and endurance
4 High, 85-95% VO_2 max., or a little above anaerobic threshold AT/TR	5-12min	2-4	5-10min	Excellent aerobic capacity and endurance, some anaerobic depending on intensity
5 Race pace	1.25-4min, total <20min	4-8	2-8min	Aerobic and anaerobic, speed endurance, pace judgement
6 Sub-maximal, 100-105% race pace	1.25-2min, Total 7.5-16min	6-8	2-3min	Aerobic and anaerobic, speed endurance, pace judgement
7 Near-maximal ALT	0.75-1.25min	10-20, often in sets	0.75-1.5min	Anaerobic, power, speed, speed endurance
8 Maximal A-LT	15-45sec	10-20, often in sets	1-2min	Anaerobic capacity, power, speed little endurance effect

Free weight or machines

Intensity	Durations of work periods	Repetitions	Length of rest	Effect
40-60% 1RM	Total<hr	15-30+ per exercise	0 (continuous circuit)	Some strength gains, aerobic endurance if work exceeds 50% VO_2 max.
60-75% 1RM	3-5 sets	10-30+	1min between sets	Strength, power and anaerobic endurance
80-90% 1RM	3-5 sets	5-10	1min 30 sec between sets	Strength/power Anaerobic endurance

1RM is the maximum weight that can be lifted once.

assess how much time is available, what the requirements and priorities are, and what is physically and psychologically possible. Regular training with adequate rest is the key to success and the right choice of quality will determine just how effective it is. Frequent and prolonged training at too low an intensity will be tiring but actually rather ineffective, whilst more intense efforts have their specific effects on the body but require sufficient recuperation.

Variety and periodization in training

Due to the specificity of training it is neither possible nor desirable to attempt to improve all aspects of performance optimally all at the same time. In the training year, or in your training and competition career as a whole, it is desirable to emphasize different aspects at different times. As a general principle the most effective system is to develop endurance first, followed by strength, before going on to more competition-specific work which will tend to emphasize speed. However, as many training effects are reversible it is best to use a mixture of methods that will maintain the qualities developed earlier. The principles governing the development of individual physical capabilities are becoming much better understood, but arriving at the precise mix which will produce the optimum performance on the most important day of competition is a much more difficult problem.

I strongly believe that training must be varied. A large number of physiological systems must be enhanced and different aspects of technique must also be developed, and this cannot be achieved by the constant repetition of one type of training. Equally, athletes need a variety of mental stimuli if they are to give of their best. Variety in training will also effectively relieve stresses on different systems in some sort of rotation, and in effect will give the systems a fuller recovery despite frequent training. Even if the Olympic training as described by Tim Foster sounds very repetitive, which to some extent it has to be to be effective, there was still variety. They rowed at different pressures, in different boats, in different places (sometimes at altitude), on ergometers; they weight trained, cycled and skied, and they raced in both heads and regattas.

Taking the year as a whole, such mixed or *complex* training is common to many sports and appears to be essential in bringing about the mixture of physical qualities necessary in our sport. If training time is limited however, we must be wary of trying to do too much at once, and in particular mixing distinctly different types of effort in one session may be counterproductive. Remember that each type of training releases its own stimulating chemicals, and we don't want mixed messages before the body has had time to adapt. Research has shown that there is a partial solution to this dilemma:

(a) Pure strength training did not improve aerobic endurance.
(b) Pure aerobic endurance work did also increase strength, but not by very much.
(c) A combination of the two types of training, following the same two schedules as for (a) and (b), gave the same strength gains as for (a) alone, as well as significant improvement in endurance – though less than when only schedule (b) was followed.

It is also worth noting that recent research has shown that a limited amount of weight training for strength has much the same long-term effect as longer sessions, and that, as well as saving time it causes much less muscle damage. This is discussed in more detail in the next chapter.

The universal solution to these problems is the *periodization* of training, within which there are defined *cycles*. In this context a cycle is a series of programmed training sessions which can be repeated over a period of time in order to achieve the desired objectives. For example, a series of six training days in a week, each day perhaps emphasizing different methods, then a slightly different following week, with the two weeks then being repeated twice a month. In such a system it is common for the quantity or quality to be enhanced slightly each two weeks so as to ensure progression. These repeated cycles make up each of the major phases of the training year:

1 Development of general ability
2 Development of specific ability
3 Competition specific.

Year on year further progression should also be planned, say over a four-year Olympic period, or through a youngster's school career.

The cyclic, or perhaps more accurately, wavelike, variation and progression of training effort and nature is common to many sports. It appears to be not only logical but physiologically sound. At any time, however, it is necessary to alternate periods of intensive effort with those of a less demanding nature. This may be day by day ('hard day, easy day' the runners say) or perhaps an easier few days each month. Training schedules of unremitting ferocity are not only potentially harmful but are demonstrably less effective. It will often be the case that the waves of recovery will be introduced before major competition when a greater emphasis on quality rather than quantity, and with more recovery time, will allow the body to adapt fully. The best training schemes must include an element of flexibility to allow *adaptation* to changing external circumstances, inevitable in an outdoor sport. In a different sense the flexibility of the schedules should also allow adaptation to the rate of progress of the athletes – and this implies regular objective measurement and assessment. Above all every session and every cycle must have clear objectives and be part of an overall plan.

We have already seen that rowing and sculling requires a very sound endurance base. To establish this base will take many hours of dedicated training and in each year such training will take up a major proportion of the time available. As a result the usual pattern for the year in the UK will be as follows:

September to January   Preparation phase, general ability – with the emphasis on the development of aerobic endurance (water and/or land training), and the development of strength and power (often through weight training).

February to April   Preparation phase, special ability – increasing quality and emphasis on speed, yet still with the retention of endurance work.

April, May   Pre-competition – maintaining endurance and developing anaerobic capacity, speed and racing techniques.

June to August   Competition specific.

As has already been stated, it is best to divide each of these periods into shorter cycles. One week could be a useful cycle but it is often found that two weeks is more satisfactory. It allows more variety; more obvious improvement will show from one cycle to the next, and it becomes easier to adopt a system with the heaviest loading in the middle of the cycle leading to an easing-off before testing, trialling or competition on the final weekend. One-week cycles are much more hectic and certainly make it much more difficult to reconcile the demands of training and racing. The pattern of the year's training and

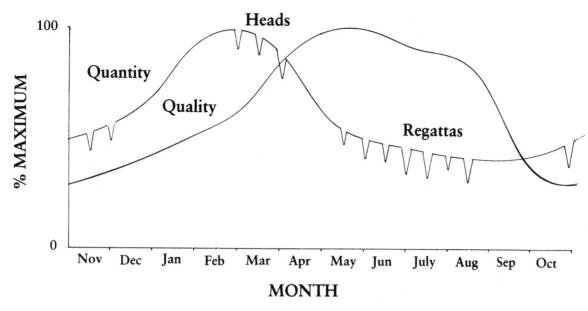

Fig. 78 Typical periodization of the training year

racing will then look something like fig. 78, sometimes referred to as the Lydiard method after the famous New Zealand coach.

It remains now to select suitable training methods to fill these cycles, based on the information in table 7, and of course depending on our objectives, the strengths and weaknesses we have to address, the time available and so on. For most of us it is only possible to absorb very tough training sessions two or three times a week, and such sessions will need to be followed by those of a less demanding nature for a day or two. If training can be carried out twice a day then it is usually best to make one of the sessions of low to moderate intensity – this will help to improve endurance still further while being less stressful. The exception to this can be when the double session comes, say, at the weekend, and can be preceded and followed by less demanding days. Similar arguments apply to combined training in one session (as was shown by the research described earlier), for example water work followed by weight training for strength. In such a case it will often be found best to carry out the lower-intensity but longer-duration work first.

During each cycle there will be some variation in both quantity and quality of work, as has already been discussed, but remembering the concept of progression, these values must increase in each subsequent cycle. In the early stages of the training year it is usual to emphasize progression in quantity first – thus building up endurance before speed, as shown in fig. 78. Early progress is often spectacular, and it may be necessary to revise ideas on rates of progress; nevertheless all increases should be gradual, and 10% per cycle is a commonly used guideline. In practice most of us are going to run into time constraints – and if we simply cannot do more we have to do it better, that is, the progression will be towards higher quality sessions. Regular testing and evaluation of progress is essential, and as a result of the evaluation, training objectives can be redefined and the training programme suitably modified.

A different problem often seems to occur after a few weeks of training when progress slows and may even temporarily reverse. To some extent this may be inevitable and simply reflect the smaller gains to be expected as bodily systems adapt, or cumulative fatigue, but there may be other physical reasons and the athlete and coach should seek to understand what might be suppressing performance. Psychologically this can be a difficult time and the athlete needs reassurance and perhaps some added variety or a new spur to motivation. Even Redgrave and Pinsent had their periods of unrewarding drudgery when their performances suffered, perhaps not surprising in view of the very demanding, very extensive and very repetitive training they undertook.

Putting together a training schedule

It is not within the scope of a book like this to provide detailed training prescriptions for all and, in any case, individual variations in ability and circumstances would make that impossible. It is notable that even in their general advice, different coaches come up with a variety of recipes based on a range of premises. Nevertheless, experience and research show that there are valuable guidelines, which are applicable to all athletes, and that there are frameworks of known efficacy on which successful schedules can be based. Before any plans can be made, however, some very basic questions must be answered:

1   What types of competition are to be attempted, when, and at what level? Just for fun, part of training, for experience – or as major competitive peaks? You may also need to consider very carefully the timing and nature of any trials or selection sessions.
2   What do these target events demand in terms of endurance, speed, technique and experience?
3   What is your present status in relation to the likely demands? It is necessary to evaluate your abilities as objectively as possible, and

reference should be made to the later part of this chapter on that topic. For overall performance you can consider past competitions or conduct time trials on the water, whilst the single most revealing land test is likely to be the ergometer. However, these are blanket measures, and at this initial stage it would be preferable to have separate estimates of endurance capacity, strength and so on in order to highlight both strengths and weaknesses. It is necessary to be realistic in judging potential, for a carthorse, however well trained, is never going to win the Derby. On the other hand be ambitious and strive for targets that at first seem far away – and especially with young athletes it is always best to be optimistic and give them every opportunity to prove themselves.

4   What are the real constraints on training time, facilities, equipment and finance? Can these constraints be overcome if necessary?

As an example, table 8 at the end of this chapter shows part of the training schedule used one spring by the St Edward's crew that later won the Schools' Head. There is a pattern to it, in accordance with the training principles outlined earlier, but it also illustrates how that pattern had to be adjusted to take account of water conditions, the desire for some early season races, and the requirement for tests and trials for potential international candidates within the crew. At this stage little concession was made to tapering or peaking for these minor competitions. You may notice that little of the work is at UT2 and this higher quality reflects three things. Firstly it shows that the crew had progressed from their winter training, and with limited time the progression was more in quality than in quantity. Secondly, their usual training water only allowed 2 or 3,000 metres before they had to stop and turn round, so the higher quality made up for that. And thirdly there was a perceived need to retain speed and to get used to higher ratings in preparation for races to come. You may also notice that weight training was usually limited to a brief supplement after work on the water, which I believe should always have first priority.

General training tips

- Don't train if you are ill, especially if you have a temperature.
- Often you may feel tired and stiff from the previous training session but this should ease as you warm up. If your muscles are

sore, actually painful even after your warm-up, then be careful, as there is a risk of doing more damage. Persistent soreness is a sign of overtraining and you should rest.

- If you have been inactive for some time, start again at a lower level and build up gradually.
- Think before training in bad weather (and consult Chapter 9) – is it worth it? Can you do something better indoors?
- Wear appropriate clothing, and keep it clean to avoid skin infections.
- Don't run in unsuitable or worn-out shoes – it is an invitation to injury.
- Good nutrition (see Chapter 9) and lots of sleep are essential adjuncts to training.
- Have plenty to drink before and after you train; take drink with you in the boat and use it frequently, especially in hot weather. Dehydration is dangerous and even mild dehydration lowers work and motivation.
- Always warm up thoroughly before any training session or race.
- Always 'wind down' gradually from any piece of work, and remember that active recovery (e.g. jogging or light paddling) is better than complete rest. Coxes have a duty to ensure that their crews do not stop abruptly after a piece of work, and coaches should choose another time at which to stop the crew for a chat!
- Weight training, particularly with free weights, is potentially hazardous and must always be overseen by a qualified instructor.
- However intense the workouts, however tired you are, never neglect technique – whether on the water, in the gym or in any other land training. Bad technique wastes energy, wastes an opportunity for its improvement, may lead to injury, and bad habits are hard to eradicate.
- Don't be afraid to ease off well before an important competition. Hard training near to the day is too late to do any good, but the fatigue can be disastrous. If in doubt, do less!
- Whatever you are doing never, ever, neglect safety precautions.

Warming up

It always takes time for our bodies to adjust to increased demands and we cannot perform well until our muscles have become warmer and our heart and breathing rates have increased. Sudden increases in effort before these preparatory changes have occurred will make you feel very breathless and tired and will increase the chances of injury. The warm-up can be carried out on land or water, but it is advisable to do both before a training session or race so that it can act as a form of technical rehearsal as well. I suggest the following scheme:

1   Jogging or other body weight exercises, or easy rowing on an ergometer, for about 10 minutes until you are warm enough to start sweating and are breathing more rapidly (some athletes find it suits them to take longer over this, particularly on the ergometer in cool weather).

2   Work through a series of stretching or Pilates exercises covering all parts of the body. The principle is to stretch slowly and then hold the stretch for, say, a count of ten before relaxing gently. Research shows that more serious stretching is best kept for after the training session when it will be more effective, but that loosening exercises are valuable before it. Further research indicates that too much stretching before a race can actually reduce performance.

3   Boat before you get cold and stiff again, and then spend anything up to half an hour working through a series of progressive technical exercises (see Chapters 2 and 3), with the most vigorous ones at the end. There is a good argument for curtailing the exposure in severe weather – either very hot or very cold.

Testing and assessment

Ultimately what matters is performance in the boat, but as already stated it is important to assess both current ability and potential objectively and regularly in various ways as an aid to effective training. The following list of common testing procedures should prove useful:

1   *Rowing ergometer*   This must be the most specific land test and its great advantage is its consistency, freedom from environmental problems and the precise monitoring that it allows of several different variables. It usually correlates very well with performance in the boat. Performance over 2,000 or 5,000 metres at set or free rate is most common, and can be combined with other measures such as heart rate. The machine can also be used to test, say, arms only as an indicator of upper body strength, or maximum speed in a few strokes

as a guide to applied strength. The physiologists can use stepped increments of work to exhaustion as a way of obtaining VO_2 max. and with the right equipment can measure lactate levels to estimate AT, and all such measures can be correlated with heart rate.

2   *Weight training for strength*   Not all coaches accept that the traditional weight training with free weights, Olympic lifts and very heavy loads is the best way to train for rowing. Those that do will probably use 1 RM, the maximum weight that can be lifted once, as the most valuable guide to personal ability on each type of lift, and the training effect depends partly on the percentage of this maximum that is used. The procedure is hazardous and it is essential that you are already very competent in lifting techniques, and have built up strength and technique for many weeks prior to any such test. Others will argue that rowers are limited in such tests as much by their technique as by their strength and that 3 to 5 RM is more valid, particularly if higher repetition training is envisaged. I do not believe that such heavy weight testing or training is appropriate for most children under 16. Personally I have come to favour higher repetition, lighter weight training in the form of a circuit as more relevant to our needs, and I note that this is what our most successful Olympic athletes have been doing. There is further discussion of these points in the next chapter.

3   *Circuit training*   There are an enormous number of forms of circuit training that we can use and which can be designed to suit our particular needs. They range from quite gentle exercises without any supplementary apparatus through to the very heavily loaded, high repetition weight circuits favoured by the best international oarsmen. Obviously, testing needs to be relevant to the particular circuit and it might take the form of timing the whole thing, or assessing performance on each exercise separately. In the latter case it is common to see how many repetitions can be completed in one minute, and then perhaps take half of that score as the training dose on each lap of a four-lap circuit.

4   *Time trials*   The problem with testing in the boat is that conditions are so important and also so variable. Side-by-side races on a fair course are particularly useful in comparing crews or scullers, and if individuals are swapped from one crew to another (seat

racing), then we can get a very good idea of who are the real boat movers. One of the snags with seat racing is that other members of the crew may not be consistent, for whatever reason, and the ideal system is when everyone thinks they are being assessed and none know who is going to move next. For absolute performance figures one hopes for still conditions, or the trials are timed in both directions and the average taken. Wind is a particular problem because a head wind slows you down more than a tail wind speeds you up; for a rough estimate take off two thirds of the time difference rather than just halving it. It is well worthwhile keeping a training diary so that a picture of progress over the weeks, months or years can be built up as you amass times for particular distances.

Illness, injury and safety

A word of warning. Overload training is intended to place the body in a state of stress, and in this condition resistance to infection can be lowered, even more so if you are overtrained. Coaches would rather their athletes were not ill and may overlook the early warning signs, and many athletes will ignore symptoms because they are highly motivated to train and compete. Training whilst infected is not just unwise but can be dangerous, and this applies particularly to viral diseases such as the common cold or 'flu. If in any doubt get good medical advice, but make sure your doctor knows what you are trying to do and is aware of the drug rules for rowing. If you are self-medicating remember to check that the potion is not on the doping list, and that even over-the-counter drugs such as Ibuprofen can have serious side effects in some circumstances. Beware of waterborne diseases such as Weil's disease and if you develop suspicious 'flu-like symptoms make sure that your doctor knows of the risk. Good hygiene is always important in minimizing the risk of skin infections, and it is usually wise to treat the water we row on as dangerously contaminated.

Frequent hard training naturally places the athlete at risk of injury, even though ours is one of the safest sports. Injuries can range from sudden traumas, with weight training being one of the most frequent causes, to chronic over-use injuries. Many injuries must be rested if the best chances of recovery are to be obtained, but this can be frustrating and difficult to accept. The only wise solution is to obtain good professional advice, if necessary from a specialist in sports injuries, and stick to it.

In both land and water training we must never compromise on safety. When on the water we must be constantly vigilant as to the danger of collision and we must not only keep a good lookout but also ensure that we obey the local water rules and any other safety regulations in force. Again we tend to be so motivated that we are prone to persuade ourselves that conditions are safe enough even when they are not. In addition we must never forget that all water sports bring the risk of hypothermia and drowning. All athletes and coxes must be able to swim well and must know, not just be told, what to do in an emergency. Coxes in particular must be well protected in cold weather and there is more on these points in the last chapter.

Examples of training schedules

Circuit training with weights

The schedule shown here was used by a successful school crew as part of their winter training. It is based on endurance work with moderate to light weights on gym machines. This method was chosen in preference to free weights for the following reasons: safety with inexperienced lifters, less time needed to set up and select weights, and better compatibility with other activities and training. Note that the circuit uses a variety of exercises and that the major muscle groups required change from one exercise to the next.

- Always stretch and warm up thoroughly first. You should be sweating before you start the circuit.
- All exercises must be done vigorously but smoothly with good technique, and through the full range of movement. Poor execution means you are wasting your time.
- Weights must always be controlled on descent. Aim for equal lift and descent time.
- This circuit should be carried out at a continuous fast pace for maximum training effect, moving swiftly from one exercise to the next.
- Build up progressively, keeping a record of your progress. Follow this order of increase, taking yourself up to 4 × 15 as soon as you can.
  1. 4 laps × 10 repetitions on all the weights
  2. 4 laps × 12
  3. 4 laps × 15

4   4 laps × 15, increasing speed
5   4 laps × 15, progressive increases in weights

The circuit

1 Shoulder laterals	keep rest of body still	12.5 kg
2 High squat-jumps	full squat, fully airborne	× 20
3 One hand seated row	pull past side of body	12.5 kg
4 Ditto	change hands	
5 Leg press	start with legs compressed	80 kg
6 Wide grip pull-down	behind head, kneeling	30 kg
7 Vertical row	knees bending, full movement	25 kg
8 Knee raise to chin	full range of movement	
9 Bench press		40 kg
10 Inclined bent knee sit-ups	hands beside head	× 20
11 Over-grasp arm curls		25 kg
12 Squat	knees at right angle	50 kg

Free weights

Before starting any free weight training with substantial loads it is essential to learn excellent technique under the supervision of a qualified instructor (see fig. 79). All sessions must be supervised and it is best to work in groups of three, with two acting as safety spotters as they rest between sets. Training loads will be set as a percentage of 1RM or 3RM as you are instructed. Start on 70%, 3 sets, 10 repetitions, increasing to 5 sets of 15 reps for strength-endurance, or increasing loads to 90% with fewer reps for greater emphasis on strength. Aim to lift weights explosively, but be very controlled on the descent, taking about twice as long.

The main lifts

1   Power clean. Lift the bar from the floor to the clean position at the shoulders in one movement. The final wrist movement of the 'clean' may be omitted if hyperextension of the back is a problem. This exercise is good for strength and co-ordination of legs, trunk, shoulders and arms.

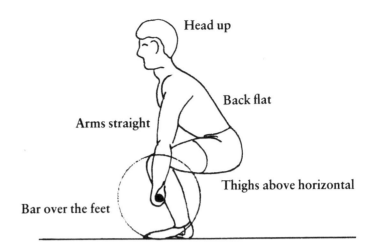

Fig. 79 The power clean is a very valuable lift, but a good starting position and good co-ordination is essential for safety and effectiveness

Head up

Back flat

Arms straight

Thighs above horizontal

Bar over the feet

2   Bench pull. A good exercise for the arms and shoulders, which protects the back because lying on the horizontal bench supports the rest of the body. This exercise is very suitable for high-repetition strength-endurance work because safe technique can be maintained despite fatigue.

3   Bench press. A safe exercise, but spotters are essential to help lift the bar on and off. Work on the antagonistic muscles helps to develop the stability and effectiveness of the upper body.

4   Squat. Either a half squat or a deep squat, in either case with the bar across the back of the shoulders or in the clean position. Although good for the thigh extensors, there are concerns about the load on the knees, especially with the deep squat, and it would be better to use a leg press machine if possible.

A final training camp

As an example of how a training schedule can be constructed for the specific purpose of peaking for a major championship, this is the schedule for the 1988 Great Britain junior men's team. It must be stressed that this was an outline only, which was intended to be modified by coaches according to circumstances, and individual needs. It was also designed to cater for a particularly high-quality group of athletes, used to training more than once a day, at a critical stage in their final preparation. By modern standards it seems to be very intensive, but it must be remembered that the racing distance then was only 1,500 metres, and the camp was to be followed by rest and very light training at the venue. Anyway it worked; the team got excellent results and Pinsent won his first World gold!

1   Technical paddle features each day and had two objectives. Firstly, the development of technique and rig both for individuals and for the very recently formed composite crews free of stress. Secondly, to provide 'active rest'.

2   The effort suggested is not constant but follows the wave principle. There is a progression through the first days to a peak on the Friday, followed by a much lighter day on Saturday. The next wave of effort begins to build on Sunday.

3   The last four days had the particular objective of time trials for the development of pace judgement. The wave principle is observed by starting and finishing with shorter distances and by increasing and then diminishing the total load.

4   Even with the most highly motivated athletes close to a clear final objective, it is desirable to provide plenty of variety – every day here is different.

The programme

Tuesday	1	Assemble boats, technical paddle
Wednesday	(i)	Steady-state 16-20 km
	(ii)	Firm paddle, stepped increases in rating
	(iii)	Technical paddle
Thursday	(i)	4 × 7 min, rate 4-6 below race rate, 6min rests
	(ii)	Fartlek, e.g. 300-stroke pyramid + starts
	(iii)	Technical paddle, some more starts
Friday	(i)	4 × 4 min, race rate, 4, 3, 2 min rest intervals
	(ii)	Steady-state 12-16km
	(iii)	Technical paddle + starts
Saturday	(i)	Technical paddle + starts
	(ii)	Free fartlek, including starts and transition to race pace
Sunday	(i)	3 (2 × 500m)
	(ii)	Technical paddle
Monday	(i)	2 (2 × 1,000m)
	(ii)	Steady state 10-12 km
	(iii)	Technical paddle
Tuesday	(i)	2 × 1,000m
	(ii)	2 × 750m
	(iii)	Technical paddle
Wednesday	(i)	Free fartlek
	(ii)	4 × 500m
	(iii)	Technical paddle

Table 8 SESBC senior squad training programme

Week	Mon	Tues	Wed	Thurs	Fri	Sat	Sun
1 (river in flood)	3K run / 20 min Ergo – AT / 3K run	Str. End. Weights / 60 min Tank	3K run / 6 × 2 min team Ergo – TR / 3K run	Str. End. Weights / 60 min Tank	3K run / 5,000m Ergo – AT / 3K run	(Gloucester canal) / 2 × 35min – UT1	–
2	3K run / 2,000m Ergo TEST / Str. End. Wts / 3K run	3K run / 16K UT2/UT1 / Sup. Weights / 3K run	3K run / 12K (VIII) UT2>UT1 / 3K run	3K run / 12K UT2 (2-) / 8K UT1 (VIII) / Sup. Weights / 3K run	3K run / 8K UT1 (VIII) / 4K fartlek / 3K run	3K run / 8K UT2 (2-) / 8K TR (VIII) / Sup. Weights / 3K run	–
3	3K run / 2,000m Ergo / Str. End. Wts / 3K run	3K run / 8K UT2 (VIII 4-) / 12K UT2/TR / Sup. Weights / 3K run	3K run / 12K UT2/UT1 (2 × 3,000m) / 3K run	3K run / 8K UT2 (4) / 12K UT2 (VIII) / Sup. Weights / 3K run	10K UT2	Race 4+ Hampton [Won]	–
4	3K run / 5,000m Ergo TEST / Str. End. Wts / 3K run	3K run / UT2/TR (2-) / 3 × 1,000m / Sup. Weights / 3K run	3K run / 12K (VIII) / 2 × 3,000m UT1 / Sup. Weights / 3K run	3K run / 8K UT2 (2-) / 10K fartlek (VIII) / Sup. Weights / 3K run	Light outing and load boat	Race VIII Henley [Won SII 3rd Overall]	–
5	3K run / Str. End. Wts / 3K run	3K run / 8K UT2 (2-) / 12K UT2/AT/TR (VIII) / Sup. Weights / 3K run	3K run / UT2/TR/ALT Inc 2 × 1,000 (2-)	12K UT2 (2-)	Light outing and load boats	Kingston Trials	Kingston Trials

7 More Advanced Ideas in Training

In the previous chapter we saw how the body responds to the demands placed upon it so that it will be better able to overcome the same load next time. If we now probe rather more deeply into this mechanism we can learn valuable lessons in how best to structure our training so that we can avoid overtraining but get the best results at the right time. The cycling coach Joe Friel said that, 'An athlete should do the least amount of the most specific training that brings continual improvement', and he goes on to say that, 'Many cyclists have become so used to overtraining that it seems a normal state'. Like all good coaches he recognizes that there is a fine line between doing the large amount of hard work that is essential for competitive success, and doing too much or the wrong things. There is no magic scientific formula that will immediately turn us into supermen, but an understanding of sports science will at least point us in the right direction. Furthermore a grasp of the jargon will enable us to make the most of new findings as they come along and pick out the parts that are most useful to us.

RESPONSE TO STRESS

When our bodies are challenged by an increase in either physical or psychological demands, or both, we react to the challenge and this reaction constitutes *stress*. As a result of the experience of stress the body releases a number of chemicals – hormones, enzymes, gene signals and so on – so that the body adapts in response, and thus the stress may be dealt with more easily on a future occasion. In our context, training and competition stresses are deliberately used to provoke adaptations that will improve performance in future. This concept of stress adaptation comes from the work of Hans Selye who defined the stress response more precisely as the *general adaptation syndrome* (GAS). This consists of three phases. The first is the *alarm reaction*, which results in the release of adrenalin and other stress hormones, which in turn increase heart rate, blood pressure, respiration and so forth. These represent the normal physiological responses to developing stress, but by themselves will produce little adaptation. The second stage is characterized by *resistance* to the stress, when the body is held in a state of readiness to meet it. When properly managed this phase is very productive of improvement in performance. The third stage is when the level of stress is so severe or maintained for so long that *exhaustion* ensues. This is potentially harmful if the exhaustion becomes chronic.

Stresses of all kinds will induce the GAS, but they tend to be rather specific in their effects – so, you can't get fitter just by worrying about it. What also matters is the sum total of stress from all the stressful influences to which the athlete is subject. It follows that the athlete's whole lifestyle will influence how much specific training stress can be tolerated, and that the well-managed training regime will seek to minimize other less productive stressors. There is no doubt that personal, social or work-induced problems may reduce training capability. Adverse weather, poor diet, disease, and lack of sleep or rest are five other potent stressors which are of great importance in determining ability to respond profitably to training.

In considering those aspects of the GAS specific to athletic training, we distinguished in the last chapter three vital principles that govern the effectiveness of the training; namely, *overload, progression,* and *specificity.*

The principle of overload is that the training load (whether in terms of strength, speed, endurance or any combination of the three) must challenge the athlete's current ability (but not necessarily exceed it). *Significant improvements will only come from significant efforts.* As a result of the overload the body will experience fatigue followed by recovery. Since the body tends to adapt to this stressful experience, the recovery will lead to an enhanced state of fitness. This is known as *over* or *supercompensation,* after the work of Yakolev and others (fig. 80). If there is no loading, or underloading, then there will be no stimulus to adapt further – indeed fitness may be lost. This concept is termed *reversibility,* and to a degree the rate of reversion will depend on the previous frequency and extent of training (fig. 81).

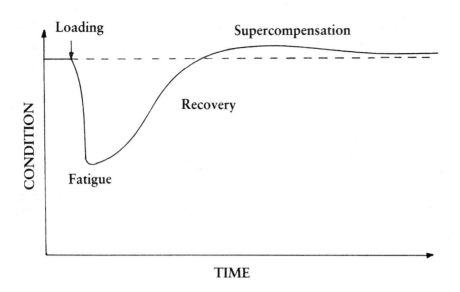

Fig. 80 The supercompensation curve (after Yakolev), showing how the body recovers to a better level of condition after a training session

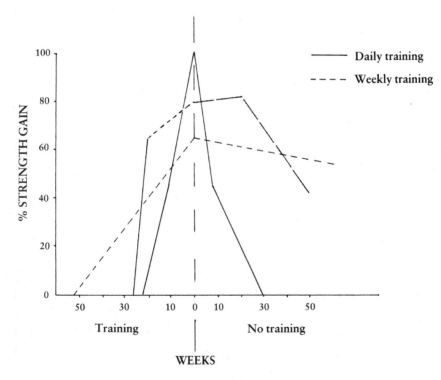

Fig. 81 Effects of weekly or daily training on strength gains or losses. Daily training brings most rapid improvement but more prolonged training enables the gains to be retained longer

It follows that as a result of supercompensation the body will require a slightly greater overload once adaptation has occurred if the same effects are to be maintained. This is what is meant by progression (fig. 82); *continual training at the same level will not bring about continued improvement.* Since loading and recovery are parts of one total process it is essential that the optimum ratio between the two is sought, and this necessarily raises the question of the appropriate frequency of training. Fig. 82a suggests a frequency whereby the new load is applied just when maximum supercompensation occurs, but there are many other possible variations. For example, it can be more effective in some circumstances to adopt a scheme based on incomplete recovery, as shown in fig. 82b, where the extended periods of stress could lead to even greater adaptation. Most training schemes for serious competition do not allow full recovery between sessions (Brendan Foster once defined an international athlete as 'someone who is always tired'). Indeed, it would be difficult to train even once daily at heavy loading on the basis of full recovery, and more usually full supercompensation will be reserved for the day of the race.

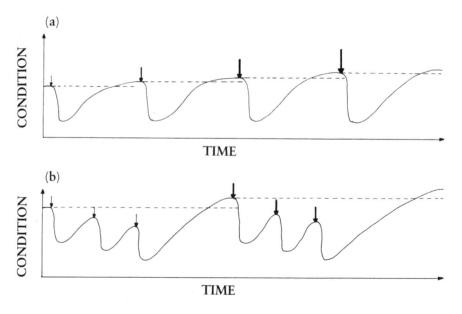

Fig. 82 Progressive overload training based on full recovery and supercompensation before the next session limits the number of training sessions (a). Alternatively, more frequent training can be used with incomplete recovery (b)

It must be remembered, however, that *rest and recovery are essential parts of the training process* and not just unfortunate human weaknesses. The physiological principle that must not be neglected is that *the body adapts to the stresses of a training session not so much during that session but more in the recovery period after it.* The wrong combination of frequency and loading will lead to a state of chronic fatigue when adaptation may fail and performance suffers. This is *overtraining.* Paradoxically, the boost to performance of an athlete who becomes a full-time professional may not lie in the extra time they might have to train but in the extra time they have to sleep and rest. When Paula Radcliffe moved up to become the world's best marathon runner much was made of her training volume and intensity (140 miles a week). This overlooked the fact that she was also famous for the amount of sleep she enjoyed and the massage, ice baths and physiotherapy that helped her recover.

Overtraining is the result of over-stressing physically or mentally, and it tends to occur in highly motivated competitors, especially those who are training themselves or whose coach's enthusiasm exceeds their physiological understanding. The symptoms are very varied but the commonest are feelings of fatigue and tiring easily which do not disperse with a few days' rest, loss of motivation, and loss of desire to train and compete. Disturbed sleep patterns, irritability, poor appetite and weight loss may all commonly occur. A more reliable indicator, particularly in young athletes, is an increase in resting heart rate of about five beats per minute for no apparent reason. More sophisticated tests will also show increases in exercise heart rate and blood pressure with slower than usual recovery, and appreciable changes in proportions of hormones.

If you are suffering from true overtraining then not only will you show these signs of great fatigue and depression but you may also be prey to greater muscle soreness, and be more prone to injury and illness. If you are showing early signs of the problem it is important to take prompt action. The first step is make sure that there is no underlying medical condition, and then to see if any other factors, such as problems at work or school, lack of sleep or poor nutrition, may be aggravating the condition. Complete rest is more effective than just reduction in training, but in severe cases it may take weeks to recover and this can be very hard to accept.

Lastly we come to the *law of specificity*, which states that, the specific adaptations or training effects are a function of the specific nature of the load. Partly this will reflect the intensity of the training stimulus – that is, what percentage of maximum strength, or speed, or endurance is demanded – but it will reflect the nature of the stimulus as well. Thus training for rowing will carry over very well to provide fitness for sculling, but the fit rower may well be unfit for, say, squash where the requirements are rather different. In general terms, extensive low-intensity work will develop endurance but not speed or strength, while brief bursts of activity with heavy weights will increase maximum strength but have little or no positive effect on endurance.

Specificity even extends more precisely to the way in which the body is used; so that, for example, lifting weights using only the outer range of limb movement will have little effect on strength at more acute angles.

EXERCISE PHYSIOLOGY

Respiration – energy for action

Vigorous exercise brings about a fall in blood pH (it becomes more acid) as first carbon dioxide and, later, lactic acid diffuse into the blood from the muscles. To some extent the acidity can be buffered (neutralized) by alkalis in the blood, but the changes will be detected by the control centres of the hind-brain. These centres stimulate an increase in the rate and depth of breathing – that is, ventilation of the lungs (V_E), as illustrated in fig. 83, dilation of the airways, and increased blood flow through the lungs as well as to the muscles. These compensatory changes tend to counteract the acidity and keep the body in a constant state at which it functions best – a concept known as homeostasis, literally 'keeping the same'. Table 9 shows some typical changes in breathed air both at rest and while rowing. Clearly, during the rowing effort, changes take place that enable a great deal more oxygen to be utilized and exchanged for waste carbon dioxide.

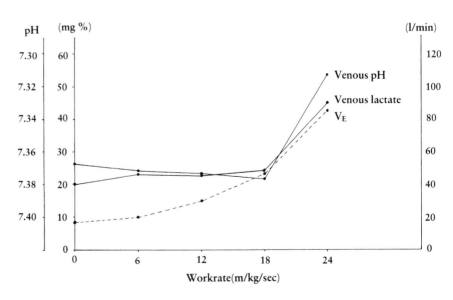

Fig. 83 With increased effort the rate and depth of breathing (V_E) increased. Beyond a critical level of effort there will be a sudden increase in lactic acid and this will increase breathing even more

Table 9 Effects of exercise on composition of breathed air

	Air breathed in %	Air breathed out At rest %	Air breathed out while rowing %
Oxygen	21	17	12
Carbon dioxide	0.04	4	9
Water vapour	variable	saturated	saturated

At higher work rates, when the anaerobic contribution to total power output exceeds about 10%, then there will be a substantial increase in both lactate and V_E, as shown in fig. 83. The highest level of exercise intensity that can be sustained without a further increase in lactate has been given various names, but the most generally accepted is the *anaerobic threshold* (AT). The values for AT are usually very high in rowers and scullers but may be even higher in other endurance sports. Above the AT there is a marked rise in V_E as well as feelings of distress brought on by the pH changes – an experienced competitor can sense the changes and adjust effort accordingly. It has been found that for many athletes the AT occurs at a blood lactate concentration of about 4.0 mmol/l. A work intensity that causes no increase in lactate above the basal level has been called the *aerobic threshold*, and since it would represent less than 60% of maximal oxygen uptake its training effect would be slight unless very prolonged. Lactate concentrations are not difficult to measure and require only a drop of blood, often from the ear lobe. Many athletes now use this test regularly in training as a guide to their work rate, and if samples are collected from the coaching launch the process need hardly interrupt the training session.

Fig. 84 shows the way in which oxygen uptake (that is, the amount of oxygen actually used by the body, not just the amount breathed) increases with workload – almost linearly at first, then curving to a plateau which represents maximal oxygen uptake for that individual (VO_2 max.). Values differ greatly between athletes and can be expressed either as absolute oxygen uptake (l/min), or in relation to body mass (ml/kg/min). Since aerobic power is so important to rowers and scullers and they are often very large people, it is not surprising that our sport has recorded some of the largest absolute values exceed-

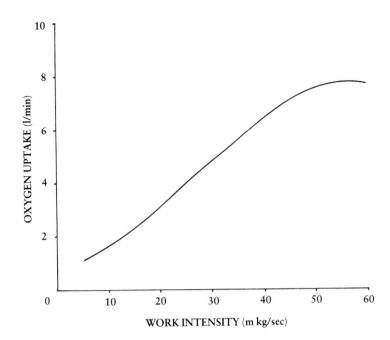

Fig. 84 Oxygen uptake increases up to a maximum with increased workload

ing 8 l/min. Values of VO$_2$ max. per kg body weight will also be very high in successful competitors despite the greater average body mass in our sport compared with most other endurance sports.

VO$_2$ max. reflects the capacity of the whole oxygen transport and utilization system – including absorption in the lungs, transport by the blood and unloading and use in the active tissues. There is a fundamental relationship between VO$_2$ max. and the endurance requirements of different sports, and even more particularly between trained and untrained people. However it is not a very good predictor within the sport – high values are a prerequisite for success, but small differences in the value do not correlate with performance. Often oxygen uptake will show dramatic improvement as untrained people improve their endurance, but this is clearly not the whole story. Values of VO$_2$ max. recorded in champion athletes have changed little in the past forty years, yet performances have improved to a much greater degree. It is probable that modern training gives better oxygen utilization by the muscles and that the muscles are themselves superior in other ways. This means that the athletes are faster and more powerful for much the same oxygen consumption. It has also been found that well-trained competitors continue to improve their performances with further training despite no further increase in their oxygen uptake.

Although for most people about 80% of their potential capacity appears to be inherited, and about 20–30% can be added by appropriate training, there are some individuals who have also inherited an exceptional ability to raise their oxygen uptake. The genes responsible are beginning to be uncovered, and even if you don't have the best ones training still makes a substantial difference to performance. All of the foregoing applies to both men and women, yet it is clear that on average women have substantially smaller oxygen uptake capacities. This seems reasonable in view of their smaller lungs, hearts and lower blood volumes, but there is another factor – the lesser amounts of lean muscle. If the values for VO_2 max. are related to lean muscle mass rather than just bodyweight, then there is little difference between men and women.

Muscle fibres differ in their structure and biochemistry, and thus their ability to use oxygen, and humans tend to have a mixture of fibre types in each muscle. To a considerable extent the mixture is genetically determined, but it can be altered by training, as can the functioning and efficiency of whatever is present. The two extreme types of fibre are known as *slow twitch* and *fast twitch* and there are various *intermediate fibres* with characteristics in between, as shown in table 10.

Table 10 Characteristics of muscle fibres

Fast twitch	Intermediate	Slow twitch
Rapid contraction speed	moderate speed	slow contraction
Fast fatiguing	moderate fatigue	fatigue resistant
Poor blood supply	moderate supply	good supply
No myoglobin (white)	some myoglobin	much myoglobin (red)
Few mitochondria	some mitochondria	many mitochondria

For our sport we need something like 70% of slow twitch fibres in our muscles because these are the ones which give us the necessary endurance. The fast twitch fibres can give extra anaerobic power, but only for a short time. The slow twitch fibres are red because they contain a profusion of blood capillaries and lots of the oxygen transferring substance myoglobin. They also have many mitochondria and the necessary enzymes for the business of aerobic respiration. The characteristics of the two extreme types of fibre can be greatly enhanced by the appropriate training, which is fortunate because we can do very little to change the proportions of each that we have inherited. It is also the case that many of our intermediate fibres can be changed by training to the characteristics that we want – for example increased numbers of mitochondria.

Desirable though it is, a high value for maximum oxygen uptake is not the whole story. In both training and competition a major factor to be considered is the percentage of VO_2 max. that can be used before anaerobic metabolism plays a major role, that is, when do we reach our anaerobic threshold? This figure is very important in sustained high performance because a high value will enable the athlete to maintain a high work rate for long periods without excessive lactate accumulation. Training can make a big difference in this respect, for an untrained person is unlikely to be able to sustain more than 60% of their (low) VO_2 max., whereas trained athletes would be able to maintain work at 80% or more of their higher uptake. We have to have both anaerobic and aerobic capacity for the 2,000 m course so we are unlikely to match the percentages of say the top marathon runners. It has been shown that training intensities close to AT (lactate concentrations of 4 mmol/l) will increase the utilization percentage even more than it increases VO_2 max.

If we refer again to fig. 75 (page 132), we see that maximum performance is gained by the addition of anaerobic power to that from aerobic respiration. We can also see that the establishment of full aerobic power takes about two minutes in a fast-starting 2,000 m race. Up till then anaerobic systems provide a high proportion of the total energy needs of the muscles, but anaerobic system II produces lactate and too much dependence on it will have a detrimental effect on the athlete. The proportion of the total energy that cannot be provided aerobically is an oxygen deficit that must be repaid later as an oxygen debt (the extra oxygen we have to breathe in and use to clear the lactate after the race). In fact some lactate will be used (for example by the heart muscle), and some will be broken down, during the race, but most of it will have to be oxidized or converted back into more useful chemicals afterwards. A good athlete might be able to incur an oxygen debt of 17 litres or more if the disposal systems are well trained. Nevertheless such oxygen debts are very painful and mental resistance to the effect is extremely important.

The need, then, is for an aerobic system with great capacity, which will reach a high level of energy production quickly and thus minimize lactate production early in the race. If the high aerobic energy generation can be maintained through the middle minutes of a race then the bulk of the energy needs will be met without excessive fatigue. The good athlete will then be able to maintain speed and still have something left for the closing stages. This is why the Olympic athletes are prepared to devote many extra hours of training to the acquisition of even very small increments of aerobic capacity. In the final minute or so of the race the contributions of the anaerobic systems can again increase, but although the total energy supply increases the aerobic part will fall. This is because the nervous stimulation of the fast twitch fibres inhibits the slower ones, and because the waste products hamper the aerobic process.

The action of breathing, and the respiratory muscles that control it, will usually be adequately trained without taking special steps. Good posture is important, for a slumped position reduces lung capacity and hinders the diaphragm and rib muscles in their movements. During the effort of rowing or sculling there is a tendency to 'press'; that is to hold the breath. This is common in weight training as well, and apart from the interruption to ventilation, high pressure builds up in the thorax. You should learn during training how to breathe freely and how best to fit the breathing rhythm with that of the stroke. There are also many good competitors who forget to breathe during the start.

A few deep breaths before the start has a calming effect and can help to ensure that the lungs are optimally charged with oxygen, but it should not be overdone. Deliberate hyperventilation (overbreathing) is to be avoided because the lowered blood carbon dioxide levels will slow breathing responses and may affect the brain and cause dizziness, tingling and cramp in the fingers, and a sense of panic. Warming up thoroughly before training efforts or races is important, for it brings about broncho-dilation and increased blood flow together with increased activation of the respiratory centre. This means that ventilation can adjust more rapidly and the 'second wind' phenomenon is reduced.

The circulatory system

The blood is a complex fluid with an enormous number of functions essential to life and high performance. It transports food and oxygen to the muscles, takes away the waste products, takes heat from the muscles and distributes it for cooling, delivers hormones, defends us from disease and so on. In order to perform these functions the blood must not only be circulated through the vessels by the pumping of the heart, but this circulatory system must be very adaptable as the demands on it vary. It is important to remember that a very significant contribution to the return of blood and tissue fluid (lymph) to the heart is made by the squeezing action of the muscles as they contract and relax. This 'muscle pump' works because veins and lymph vessels have one-way valves in them, thus preventing back-flow in this low-pressure part of the system. Maintenance of the muscle pump is one of the main reasons for winding down gradually after an effort.

During a hard rowing effort the heart rate and stroke volume (the amount of blood pumped at each beat) will both increase so that the total cardiac output rises from about 6 l/min at rest to over 30 l/min, as shown in fig. 85. A number of automatic mechanisms govern this response including the same fall in blood pH that causes our breathing to increase as well. Under extreme stress a maximum heart rate of over 200 beats per minute may be reached, with maximal stroke volume of 160–180 ml usually achieved at about 160 bpm. Work at this exhausting level will be in excess of the AT and therefore large amounts of lactate will be accumulating. Responding to the pH change and the higher ratio of CO_2 to O_2 detected in the arteries, the brain will cause blood vessels in the muscles to dilate, and others (such as the gut) to constrict, so that the flow of blood to the muscles will be enormously

Fig. 85 Both heart rate and total heart output increase rapidly at the beginning of a race and then stabilize at a high level. When the rate goes up again in the final sprint there may not be time for the heart to fill completely, so output falls

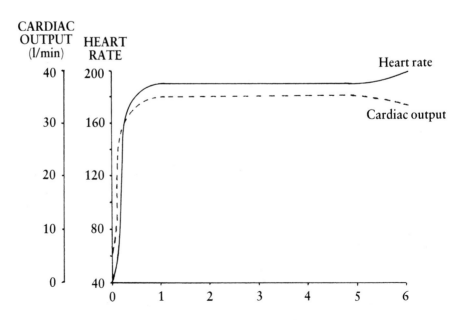

increased. Core body temperatures will rise by several degrees and more blood will be diverted to the skin for cooling, until perhaps extreme exhaustion sets in when the blood may be temporarily withdrawn.

All these adjustments take time, and particularly in the first minute of a race or demanding piece of training the ability of the circulation to meet the body's aerobic needs will lag behind the muscles' energy use. Consequently, carbon dioxide and lactate will tend to accumulate and lead to feelings of distress, which then lessen as the improved circulation clears away these waste products and brings more oxygen. This is the 'second wind', and since many of the responses can be invoked in advance it is clear that a thorough warm-up is essential and will reduce the second wind effect. The good competitor will learn that the subjective feelings of weakness can be ignored and that this may be a good time to maintain the pressure on the opposition.

During the recovery after the effort the heart rate will fall very rapidly at first, yet the various factors described earlier have hardly had time to change; pH is still low, lactate and CO_2 are still high, and so on. The reduction in rate is so rapid that it must be largely due to changes in stimulation of the heart by the nerves, originating in the brain elsewhere than the fully automatic cardiovascular centres. The feeling of relief at the end of an effort may well be associated with this phenomenon. The converse is also true – apprehension before the start causes sympathetic stimulation of the heart and adrenal glands and other well-known symptoms including high heart rate. Anyone who thinks that our Olympic champions are immune from such pre-race nerves should read Matthew Pinsent's candid accounts of his great races.

After a minute or two the pulse recovery will slow and the heart rate will often level off before slowly declining again (fig 86). Here we are seeing the true signs of metabolic recovery. After a brief and not too exhausting piece of work the rate may be back to its resting level within about five minutes, but more extensive effort will require much more recovery time and the raised metabolic rate may demand more from the heart for many hours. Several fitness tests (for example the Harvard Step Test) rely on measures of heart rate recovery after exercise as indices of fitness, but such tests seem to work best with less highly trained or even untrained people and they are not designed for testing recovery from maximal effort.

Endurance training has beneficial effects on the circulatory system. Substantial intermittent or continuous efforts with large muscle groups lasting more than one hour, will give the greatest enlargement of the

Fig. 86 A typical heart rate recovery curve after a hard but not exhausting effort

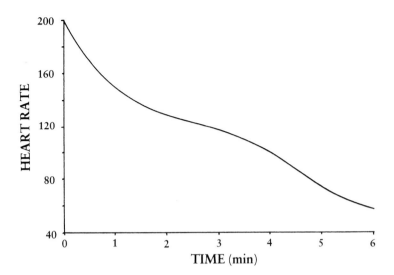

heart and will also improve muscle capillarization very substantially. Reference to the training information in the previous chapter will show that such training will also have very important effects on muscle endurance and VO_2 max. Other types of very intense training, for example weight training for strength, will certainly raise the heart rate repeatedly but do not have the same long-term effects on the heart or vessels.

As we have already seen, training loads should be related to the athlete's aerobic capacity and anaerobic threshold, where possible, but in practice these may not be easy or convenient to measure. Fortunately there is usually a good relationship with heart rate and it is easy to monitor heart rates and use these as an objective guide in training (see Table 5 in the previous chapter, page 138). Taking the pulse at wrist or throat is simple but can be very inaccurate at high rates as well as impractical in motion. Heart monitors that detect electrical signals from the heart via chest electrodes are the best, and those that store the data for later downloading and processing are very valuable. Fig. 87 charts the heart responses obtained in this way of a junior international rower during a particularly demanding training session.

As a useful rule of thumb, the pulse rate range that will give a good training effect in continuous work will be 150–180 bpm, but the duration of the work will need to exceed 30 min at least three times a week if any progress is to be maintained. In the absence of more precise estimates of VO_2 max. and AT, the following calculation is commonly quoted for the minimum heart rate for any training effect.

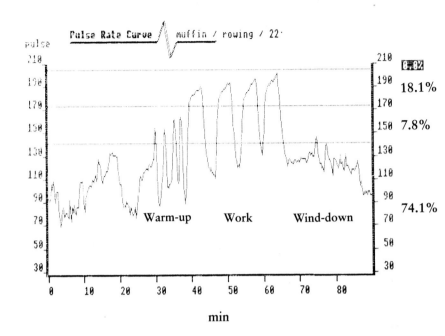

Fig. 87 The result of continuous monitoring of the heart rate during a training outing when the work was four 4-minute rows with diminishing rest intervals. The dotted lines across the graph are estimates of (from top) maximum heart rate, anaerobic threshold, and training threshold

Maximum heart rate (MHR) = 220 – age in years
Heart rate reserve (HRR)   = MHR – resting heart rates
Effective training threshold = 60% HRR + resting HR
(Estimates of MHR are usually imprecise, so it would be better to
   measure your own with a heart-rate monitor)
Example: a 25-year-old with a resting pulse of 45 bpm
MHR = 220–25 = 195
HRR = 195–45 = 150
Training threshold = 150 × 60/100 + 45 = 90 + 45 = 135 bpm

Other physiologists suggest that MHR is more accurately estimated by taking 214 – (80% × age), but in truth both methods can give errors of up to 20 bpm, so it hardly seems worth the extra arithmetic! We are all different, but if you use a heart rate monitor you will soon find your real maximum, and you will also be able to judge how the sensation of breathlessness at AT equates to a particular rate.

In intermittent intense training, especially with weights, the heart rate may be higher than the oxygen uptake would seem to justify. In one study the heart rate was 155 bpm but no endurance training occurred because oxygen uptake under these conditions was only 45% VO_2 max. It is thought that in such cases extra hormonal influences and disproportionate lactate production elevate the heart rate.

True interval training was developed in the 1930s by Gerschler and Reindell specifically as a heart and circulation training method. They found that repeated fast but sub-maximal runs of about 200 metres, which raised the heart rate to 180 bpm, interspersed with recovery periods which allowed the rate to fall to 120 bpm, had the greatest effect on the heart. It seems that the heart is expanded as a result of the maximal stroke volume occurring during the recovery period. Karl Adam adapted these methods for rowing and showed that 500 metres (or 10% more for fast eights) was the optimal distance. This would be repeated six times with a 2–3 min recovery paddle to bring the pulse down to 120 bpm. Adam also used longer repetitions of 1,000 metres or more. Subsequently, in both running and rowing, Lydiard and others had much success with high continuous mileage as the long-term foundation before the shorter, faster repetitions nearer the time of competition. Now that international athletes devote more time to their training, and women and juniors are racing over 2,000 metres, short interval training is less commonly used.

Adaptations built up by more extensive work may be slower to show fruit, but do seem to be more durable and more effective in altering muscle capillarization and metabolism. There was a time when 'Long Slow Distance' (LSD) was the favoured method, but for most of us with limited time, better results are likely from a judicious mix of, and periodization of, extensive higher quality work and faster repeated pieces. Even supposing that we decide that we are going to row 20 miles a day it would be better to do that as two 10-mile sessions at higher quality with a rest in between. This is what marathon runners would do, although for their specific purpose they would run the non-stop 20 perhaps once a week. Valuable though endurance training is, it must be balanced against the need for some speed retention throughout the year. The danger lies in turning the athlete into an 'endurance stereotype' who is unable to respond to the intensity of a 2,000-metre race. One marathon champion said that he 'trained for endurance until he couldn't jump' – well, we need our explosive power!

Causes of fatigue

It is commonly assumed that the major cause of all muscle fatigue is lactic acid, and although this may be true for a 2,000-metre race there are other factors that are significant during the race and will also be encountered during training, preparation for races and during recovery. In longer

Fig. 88 Exhaustion at the end of a very hard race. St Edward's win the Princess Elizabeth at Henley in 1984. (Photograph by Chris Morgan)

distance races, say up to about 20 minutes, lactic acid will still be the major limit to performance for the well-prepared competitor – although the few very long races, such as the Boston Marathon, will create rather different problems. Some of the causes and effects of fatigue take a long time to disperse and tend to be cumulative, but knowledge of them can help you to minimize them. In the discussion of the separate causes which follows it will be seen that some are specific to muscle, whilst others affect different tissues or are more widespread through the body. Understanding the problems should help us to avoid them – know your enemy!

Lactic acid

The problem with lactic acid is not that it is a specific poison – indeed it can be used as fuel by heart muscle – but that it is an acid. Other acids will have similar unwelcome effects and this includes the carbonic acid formed when carbon dioxide from respiration dissolves in the tissue fluids and plasma. Acids release positively charged particles called *protons* that will combine with negatively charged substances known as *bases* (alkaline) to become neutral *salts* (such as lactate). A scale of values called the pH number indicates the acidity or alkalinity of a solution, where pH 7 is neutral, higher numbers indicate bases or alkaline solutions and lower numbers indicate increasing acidity. There are large amounts of bases in the blood and tissue fluids so the pH of those fluids is slightly alkaline at about 7.35 at rest, but we are very sensitive to any change either way and it is a major factor in the control of heart rate and breathing.

Much of the fatigue-inducing effect of acids such as lactic acid is that the protons they produce interfere with the chemistry of the muscles and also the nervous system controlling the muscles. Some lactate is present in the body at all times but when the production rises after the anaerobic threshold has been exceeded then the pH will fall (see fig. 83 earlier). We have seen that lactic acid is the product of anaerobic respiration in the skeletal muscles, so intense efforts that recruit a high proportion of fast twitch fibres will cause a rapid increase in acidity and rapid fatigue. Skeletal muscles cannot use or break down lactate or lactic acid very rapidly, although heart muscle and the liver in particular can, so excess production is passed into the tissue fluid. The acid then has a deleterious effect on the muscle as a whole before passing into the bloodstream and having more widespread effects. Improved circulation in and around the muscle as a result of training will help to remove the lactate more rapidly and training will also enhance the mechanisms that dispose of it. About one fifth of the lactate will be respired and the rest can be reconverted to glucose by the liver when more oxygen is available (hence the repayment of the oxygen debt after the race).

Rowing and sculling uses large muscle groups very extensively and if about 30% of those muscles are fast twitch fibre then there is considerable potential for lactate production. The 70 kg body contains about 47.5 litres of fluid, so the overall change in lactate and pH in a race (table 11) does not seem very much, but it is critical. The effects of the acid are reduced by the presence in both muscle and blood of *buffers*, that is, bases such as hydrogen carbonates which can 'mop up' excess protons. The buffers in muscle can deal with maximum lactate production for only about 10–15 sec, but there is a larger reserve in the blood.

Table 11 Changes in lactate and pH during rowing competition

Race distance	Resting	500m	2,000m	40,000m
Blood lactate (mmol/l)	0.7–1.8	30–34	20	6–12
Blood pH	7.35–7.45	6.8–6.9	7.0	7.15–7.25

Clearly it is advantageous to maximize aerobic energy production and delay the highest lactate levels in a race until the end. The tactics that will help with this are discussed in Chapter 8, whilst the methods and rationale for improving oxygen supply have already been given. As far as the muscles themselves are concerned, the training needs to emphasize the development of the oxygen-using fibres, but so crucial is the contribution of anaerobic power to a fast pace that its parallel development must not be neglected. Experience of work under high lactate levels is not only an essential stimulus to the enhancement of biochemical processes to alleviate its effects, but is also important in improving co-ordination under this stress. Acidosis is painful and disturbing, so repeatedly overcoming its baleful effects during training is also most important from a psychological point of view. When asked when it started to hurt during the Olympic final, James Cracknell replied, 'Just after the start!'

We have seen that high lactate levels take a long time to disperse and therefore anaerobic training should be curtailed immediately prior to competition. The wise competitor will also attempt to use minimal lactate tactics in preliminary races by maintaining a steady pace and avoiding a sprint finish. Winding down after a training effort or race is also important, for it helps to maintain blood flow and tissue fluid exchange in the muscles and hence flushes out acid residues more quickly.

Glycogen

For most race distances except the very long ones, the primary fuel for muscle contraction will be glucose, despite the ability of the fibres that form the majority in the athlete's muscles to use fatty acids as well. This glucose will come from glycogen (a larger storage molecule made up from glucose sub units) stored as granules in the muscle fibres. An untrained person might store about 300 g of glycogen in the muscles and a further 100 g in the liver; a well-trained and rested athlete might have more than 600 g in the muscles. This glycogen can be quickly converted to glucose when needed. Blood glucose (blood sugar) contributes little to muscle contraction in the early stages of exercise or in a short race; indeed there are mechanisms to ensure that it does not, for it must be spared as the essential fuel for the brain and nervous system. Although blood sugar does eventually fall during prolonged hard exercise, this should not be an important cause of muscle fatigue in our races but it can affect the overall sensation of fatigue (fig. 89). It follows that attempts to boost blood sugar immediately before training or competition by eating or drinking glucose will have little or no positive effect on the muscles, and as explained in Chapter 9 may even be deleterious to performance.

Fig. 89 Blood glucose levels do not fall unless duration of a mild effort is greater than one hour

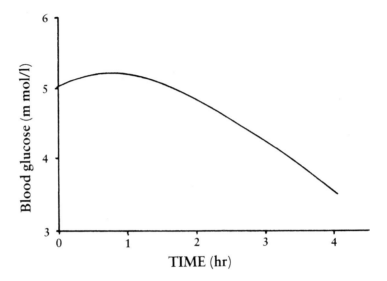

The usual stores of muscle glycogen are likely to be adequate for all but the longest races, and the exhaustion of glycogen is most unlikely to be the cause of fatigue in the few minutes of a 2,000-metre race unless they were already severely depleted. High initial levels of glycogen do help in biasing muscle chemistry towards maximum rates of energy production. In long races or prolonged training sessions, depletion of glycogen reserves does become an important cause of fatigue, and this is what marathon runners call 'hitting the wall' and cyclists term 'the bonk'. In these circumstances the body will tend to use more fat, putting more emphasis on the slow twitch (aerobic) fibres and increasing oxygen requirements as well. Once the glycogen stores are used up, say after one or two hours of hard work, sustained performance can only be at a very much-reduced level.

It should be remembered that anaerobic respiration uses glucose (and hence glycogen) very rapidly to produce a small yield of energy, and that the lactate formed will only slowly be reconverted. Thus intense efforts will deplete glycogen reserves much more rapidly and this could be a problem after repeated training efforts or a series of races close together. Even lower intensity sustained effort will lower the levels and it is important to appreciate that replenishment from the diet is slow. Although dietary adjustments are helpful (see Chapter 9), it is likely that repeated hard training will keep glycogen stores low and will lead to poor fatigue resistance. Rest, and recovery of glycogen levels, is therefore vital before important competition and is part of 'supercompensation'. Glycogen is stored with extra water, so good hydration is also important, but very large stores will give a sensation of stiffness in the muscles as well as adding extra weight – the full business of 'carbohydrate loading' is therefore rarely desirable in rowing.

Most people find that strong coffee reduces general fatigue and helps performance, and this is partly due to effects on muscle metabolism. Caffeine not only combats the sensation of fatigue through its effects on the nervous and hormonal systems, but it also affects fat metabolism – releasing fatty acids into the bloodstream and encouraging their use by the muscles. Whilst this spares glycogen and increases endurance it may not be what is required for high-speed rowing. Large amounts of caffeine have effects that may hamper performance and, although it is no longer on the list of banned drugs, its use should be approached with caution.

Electrolytes and water

During exercise water and minerals are lost in sweat and water is lost through breathing. Sweat is much more dilute than blood plasma so the major loss is water (see Chapter 9). Surprisingly the concentration of the body fluids changes little and this is particularly important in the cases of sodium, potassium, calcium and magnesium, which are lost in sweat and are essential for the muscle contraction mechanism. They will have to be replaced perhaps by drinking electrolyte solutions during or after the session or from the diet afterwards. During hard efforts these ions move from the muscles into the tissue fluid and blood and in the short term there should be enough in reserve. In the longer term, significant losses or imbalances of these minerals or just a change in their concentration will contribute to fatigue and may cause further problems of cramp, loss of co-ordination, mental confusion and even complete collapse.

Very large amounts of water can be lost through sweating in addition to that passing out of the body in breath and in urine. Dehydration is serious, not just because of the marked drop in performance as a result of even a 2% loss of body water, but because of the potential dangers of collapse, overheating and even death (see Chapter 9 for further details). Water loss affects performance in two main ways: through changes in the critical concentration of substances dissolved in the blood, and through the increased viscosity of the blood making it harder to circulate. As it happens, too much water can also cause problems because it dilutes the body fluids too much.

Phosphates are essential in transferring energy to the contracting muscle proteins, and in some types of fatigue phosphate leaks out of the muscle and into the tissue fluid and blood. In the laboratory, bathing the fatigued muscle cells in phosphate does help to restore them. It has been found that drinking phosphate solution before training helps performance but this is thought to be due to a different effect enhancing oxygen carriage by the blood. Since the long-term effects of such procedures are unknown it would be unwise to experiment.

Nervous system

Many changes occur in the nervous system as a result of the stress of hard training or racing and these changes cause both some aspects of fatigue itself and the sensations of fatigue (not necessarily the same thing!). The nervous system works not just by the nerve impulses that it transmits but also by the release of a range of chemicals (*neurotransmitters*) at its junctions, terminals and connections. At the nerve/muscle junction a transmitter chemical is released to cause changes within the fibres which then trigger the sequence of events leading to contraction. Numerous reports over the years suggest that at intense workloads this communication system may fail, and then the muscle will not contract optimally. As muscle fibres become fatigued, from whatever cause, then the number recruited at any one time will rise from the usual 30% to 70% or more. This means that each muscle motor unit gains less rest before it has to contract again and therefore fatigue increases rapidly. At this stage the electrical activity in the muscle becomes intense, causing marked tremor before collapse.

The brain uses a large number of neurotransmitters, some of which dictate mood and wakefulness and others which are responsible for sensations of pain and fatigue. Some of these neurotransmitters appear in the blood and it is reported that when rats are exercised to exhaustion on a treadmill, and then their blood is injected into fresh rats, the fresh ones fall asleep! Many neurotransmitters are related to amino acids present in the blood and there is evidence that diet or specific supplements can help reduce fatigue symptoms. Not all substances can cross the blood/brain barrier, but of course there are drugs, including caffeine, which can reach the brain and reduce the sensation of fatigue.

Temperature

An active muscle produces a lot of heat and quite quickly warms up by 2–3° C or more at its centre with beneficial effects. The viscosity of the muscle is reduced, so making it easier to move, the transference of oxygen is more thorough, and enzymes are speeded up. There is no doubt that warm muscles are more efficient – as much as 40% more – but if temperatures rise further the enzymes and other proteins will be adversely affected as may be the nervous system. Thus high internal temperatures can be a cause of fatigue. Further effects of heat and their avoidance are discussed in Chapter 9.

Vitamins

Some vitamins are essential in energy production in the muscles; others are needed for blood components. For example, B-complex vitamins are involved in aerobic respiration chemistry within the muscle cells and elsewhere. It is most unlikely that race fatigue will be due to depletion of these vitamins during the race, but if the athlete is deficient in them beforehand then early fatigue is probable. Of course if you are not deficient then taking in more will do no good. This subject is discussed more fully in relation to diet in Chapter 9.

Training for specific qualities

Strength and power

Strength is the muscles' ability to exert force and overcome a resistance, whereas power includes the speed of the work done. The two attributes seem to be related, especially in the work of rowing where the ability of the muscles to overcome the wind and water resistance quickly is likely to be a function of the strength available. However in practice it is found that power (especially if it is to be sustained) and absolute strength are not very closely correlated and require different training regimes having different effects on the muscles. This power should be distinguished from speed *per se,* which is a different quality again with some different origins particularly in the nervous system.

The strength of a muscle is ultimately dependent on the number of fibres, their size and their nature – fast twitch being the stronger. Very roughly, the strength of a muscle is dependent on its cross-sectional area, giving a force of 3–4 kg/cm^2. The fibres are grouped together in *motor units* and the strength achieved will also depend on the number of these contractile units actually recruited, and that is the province of the nervous system and how it activates them. Both the size and the activation of the muscle are susceptible to training.

After a course of specific strength-training the muscle will be larger in cross-section – this is *hypertrophy.* Some of the hypertrophy is the result of increases in non-contractile elements such as blood vessels but primarily it comes from the increase in size of the muscle fibres – *not* from any increase in their number. Initially the hypertrophy may be masked by a reduction in fat. In untrained subjects the increase in cross-sectional area occurs in the later weeks or months of a strength-training programme when heavier weights are being tackled, and is very marked; it is less obvious in those with a greater training background. In the early stages of both strength and power training, there is a very rapid increase in force without any appreciable increase in muscle size. This is due to improvement in the nervous control of the muscles; that is, there is a reserve of strength that can be mobilized by appropriate training.

The specificity of the training regimen is vital. Elite weightlifters, who are undoubtedly stronger, do not necessarily have as great a muscle mass as elite body builders do. And power training, with the emphasis on explosive, fast movements, even with substantial resistance, may not lead to any great hypertrophy at all (fig. 90). The essential requirement for hypertrophy is that the training load is near to maximal and the stimulus is lengthy. This implies very heavy resistance training at slow speeds. Development of maximal strength follows the same rules, i.e. a load of between 80 and 100% of the current maximum for a single lift (1RM) and lifted steadily rather than explosively. Such a load will probably limit repetitions to between one and five per

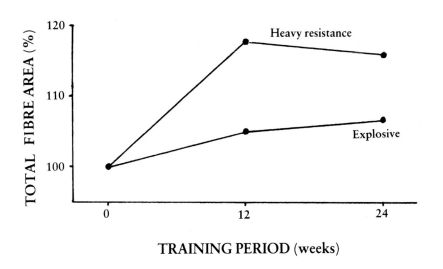

Fig. 90 Muscle hypertrophy depends on the type of training

set. Prolonged training of this nature will produce little additional gain in strength and will tend to reduce the ability to overcome the resistance quickly. For rowing it would be better to use loads that allow five to ten faster repetitions in each of three to five sets. It is usual in strength training to allow generous rest between sets, but some very successful coaches advocate a much more intense system with limited rest. This will give strength endurance benefits, but there are dangers in trying to work fast with heavy loads when fatigued. We should also remember the recent research which shows that just one set gives much the same benefit, but with less muscle damage.

It is debatable anyway how useful maximum-strength training is for rowing, for it would seem that more dynamic methods are more appropriate for the specific needs of our sport. It is worth noting that dynamic training, working against substantial resistance but with more repetitions performed briskly, will increase muscle power without a large increase in muscle mass and body-weight. If carried out as a circuit then some muscle groups can gain a useful rest whilst others are being used and there is no need for further rests between sets.

Although there are few hard facts to rely on, there is still debate as to the relative merits of free weights and resistance-training machines. It is unlikely that resistance provided by springs or elastic will be generally useful for our purposes because of the way in which the resistance increases with extension, though it may have some particular value in strengthening that part of the range of movement. Most machines use weights lifted against gravity by levers, wires or pulleys and some devices are arranged to give a more complex effect. It is commonly said that a free weight movement, such as the power clean, is particularly valuable because it involves a co-ordinated use of many muscle groups, including those for balance and stability. It is questionable whether such 'Olympic' lifts really are close enough to the rowing action, but they are difficult to mimic with most forms of apparatus. One of the snags with free weight lifts is that they do reward skill, and for many non-specialist lifters this skill is the true limit to their performance (especially for 1RM), which in turn means that training is not at optimum muscle tension. Machines do not require so much skill and have the added advantage that training can be targeted more precisely to particular muscle groups. There is no doubt that training on machines is potentially much safer, and this alone must be a major consideration.

Examples and advice for both methods of resistance training are to be found in Chapter 6.

A further point of specificity needs to be remembered, in that the gains will be largely restricted to the range of movements used in training. The training regime must cover the full range of limb and trunk movements used in rowing and sculling. We need to be wary of any training that does not at least resemble some part of the rowing action, so, for example, most isometric training methods will clearly be of little value.

Endurance

In rowing and sculling there is a requirement for endurance of both aerobic and anaerobic systems simultaneously, and this presents a particular challenge in training. The stress of training sends rather specific chemical messages to our muscles, heart, blood vessels and so on to adapt to meet that stress – trying to train both aerobically and anaerobically in the same session sends mixed messages and may mean that neither is fully effective. It is now well established that the best answer is to develop aerobic endurance first (and in any case it takes longer), and then to hone the anaerobic component nearer the time of competition. General endurance – the ability to continue a low workload for a very long time – is of limited value in our sport, and specific training with that end solely in mind seems a waste of time. Higher-quality work will in fact be more productive of useful endurance anyway. What we really need is improvement in power endurance, and the specificity rules show that the speed, force and duration of the work need to be progressively increased and matched to requirements.

There are some typical muscular changes as a result of aerobic endurance training which not only alter the characteristics of some of the fibres but also increase capillaries, mitochondria and glycogen stores – all of which will improve muscular endurance. There is a good correlation between these muscle factors and the standard measure of whole body aerobic capacity known as VO_2 max. However, it is also important to note that muscle endurance capacity can still be improved even with no further increase in VO_2 max., as was shown earlier. Up to a point, greater anaerobic capacity can be added to the aerobic, and here we are looking to enhance the systems for disposing of lactate, buffering lactic acid and training the nervous system and psyche to cope with the unpleasant effects.

Co-ordination

Most of the problems of co-ordination in rowing and sculling are the business of the nervous system, but there are some muscle factors involved as well. The rowing and sculling actions require the precisely controlled contractions and relaxations of a very large number of muscles, as well as the correct patterns of recruitment of motor units within those muscles. For optimum co-ordination the force, range and speed of all the movements should be trained to the requirements of the racing stroke. Resistance training methods are often suspect on this score and additionally tend to neglect the antagonistic muscles as well as cause uneven fatigue of muscle groups. Even after water or ergometer training, muscle fatigue can have important consequences for co-ordination because not all the rowing muscles will fatigue to the same extent simultaneously. The usual result is weird compensatory movements. Although it is sometimes necessary to train to the point of extreme fatigue, it is very important to strive always to maintain correct technique – thus the training will be most effective and bad habits will not become established.

The rowing or sculling action has to be learnt, and although it is based upon pre-existing reflexes and motor pathways, they have to be modified, co-ordinated and overlaid with more voluntary actions. Repetition of the actions over a long period tends to make them more automatic. This learning process is very much dependent upon the alteration or conditioning of reflexes, so that they become conditional reflexes. Many of the repetitive movements of our sport will be controlled more or less automatically this way, yet the basic technique must still be responsive to change. For example, rowing in rough water requires changes in hand heights, or gusts of wind may present novel balance problems. At first, the response will involve much conscious activity and be slow and clumsy, but with experience the modified reflexes are brought into play much more smoothly and quickly. After long-term training there will be adaptations to the memory system even in the spinal cord. The cautionary part of this is that wrong movements can be learnt just as easily – and they are very difficult to unlearn. Remember, practice makes permanent not perfect!

Speed

The speed of muscle contraction required in rowing is not as high as in some other sports, but quick, deft movements are required, particularly at the catch. It is important that training should be carried out at relevant speed and the case has already been made for emphasizing speed in resistance training so that power rather than just maximal strength is developed. The increased speed of a boat through the water is largely achieved by increases in power, but especially at the start very high-speed movements are required for effective use of that power. If some training is carried out at greater than normal speeds then the quickness and co-ordination that is required will be developed further. The principle is to use short, repeated bursts of low-load, high-speed work, and on the water it may be helpful to shorten the stroke while doing this.

Flexibility

Modern technique requires a large range of movement, which should be attainable without strain and without stiffness. It is commonly believed that heavy resistance training in particular will limit such flexibility ('muscle-bound'), but this is unlikely to be true in our sport though it might be for some very hypertrophic body-builders. It has already been stated that for other reasons strength training should be over the whole range of movement and this will clearly aid mobility.

The development of greater flexibility and stability should be a key part of the training programme and suggestions were made in the previous chapter as to warm-up and stretching exercises which will aid this. Muscles contain a considerable amount of connective tissue and regular stretching will help to increase its length and elasticity. The range of movement of joints is also limited by the connective tissue around them and this too is amenable to improvement by stretching exercises. All these tissues contain *stretch receptors* that monitor the elongation and give vital feedback to the nervous system, and one of the effects of stretching is to reduce their inhibitory effects on the extent of movement.

In order to use our big muscle groups effectively through a full range of movement we need the help of a very large number of other muscles, principally in the trunk, that support, stabilize and firmly link the body parts. This is what is meant by *core stability* and although the other training will help to develop this asset it is still worthwhile incorporating additional exercises into the schedule with this specific aim in mind. One of the obvious signs of fatigue is deterioration in posture, and then technique is lost and even greater fatigue ensues – so endurance and strength in the postural muscles has a very important role to play. Finally, we must not forget the value of flexibility and core support in preventing injury. For example, good tone in the abdominal muscles helps to maintain good posture and support for the lower back, and flexibility of the hamstrings is essential for the correct movement of the pelvis, which again helps protect the lower back.

Motivation

Training hard enough and long enough to be successful in this demanding sport is not easy, and inevitably there will be times when it does not seem to be working or no longer seems to be worth the effort and sacrifices. This is the time to remind yourself of your goals and ambitions and to think about the ultimate rewards. Keep a training diary and look back over the progress already made, be determined not to waste it and make sure that you have realistic targets always in view. Perhaps the greatest encouragement is a successful racing programme, and this aspect is dealt with more fully in the next chapter. It is particularly hard to cope with tough times if you are on your own, and without a doubt the support and encouragement of a knowledgeable coach is of

Fig. 91 The Italian lightweight four celebrate their victory in front of their home crowd at the World Championships in Milan. Motivation enough?

immense value. It matters too that your family and friends, school or colleagues are supportive, but if not, the best answer to your critics is to be determined to show them that they are wrong.

MASTERS ROWING AND SCULLING

Masters are subject to exactly the same physiological rules as younger athletes. However, it is generally true that their adaptations to training will be slower and their recovery times longer than in their youth. Eventually the effects of ageing will exceed the benefits of training and performance will decline. Nevertheless, the training precepts outlined will continue to give benefits and help to maintain health and quality of life even into very old age.

As we age our maximum heart rate declines, our blood vessels lose flexibility and responsiveness (and may be partially blocked), and our muscles lose bulk and strength. In addition our joints and connective tissues degenerate and cause loss of flexibility and mobility. These changes can be minimized by continuing strength and mobility programmes. Anaerobic thresholds become lower and tolerance of higher quality training is reduced – thus even more emphasis should be given to aerobic work on the water and ergometer. The maintenance of appropriate training and diet will help to delay and reduce the rate of performance decline.

8 Racing

I imagine that for most readers of this book racing will be the ultimate aim of their involvement with rowing or sculling. However much we may enjoy being out on the water or the camaraderie of our club mates, the reason why we seek to optimize our equipment and training is to perform better in races. For some of us true satisfaction will only come from winning races at the highest level, and for others it is the fun of simply taking part but feeling that you have given a good account of yourself. One of the great joys of our sport is that we can pit ourselves against all-comers in competitions of several sorts, and that the sport is organized in such a way that we can compete fairly against others of a similar standard and yet still be part of a continuum stretching up to international level. Even if we are very well prepared in other ways there is no doubt that getting the best out

Fig. 92 Six hundred metres into the final of the Junior World Championships at Vichy and the coxed pairs are jockeying for position

of ourselves when it matters in a race is an additional skill which we need to practise and learn. We should choose our races with care, prepare for them thoroughly, and make sure that everything is right on the day.

DECIDING ON A COMPETITION PROGRAMME

Unless we are only competing for fun I think that we should have some competitive peak or goal to aim for both in the long and short term. In this way we can structure and plan our development and use targets to motivate us and to measure our progress. I do believe that racing should be both enjoyable and useful, so that we can derive pleasure and valuable lessons from it, for surely that is the whole point of the exercise. I have always believed that we should race as often as can be justified. On the other hand it is certainly possible to race too often and as a result be unable to recover and to maintain form or be unable to fit in enough training to make best progress towards a further goal. We should also bear in mind that it is very difficult to reach peak form more than once or twice in a year. Perhaps paradoxically we do not have to expect to win every time out, since racing for experience or to measure ourselves against better opposition can still be rewarding, and many competitors treasure memories of hard fought but losing races above the easy victories. The way in which the GB coxless fours responded to their defeats in Lucerne before going on to win the Olympic titles in Sydney and Athens illustrates how even those cathartic experiences could be the vital spur to ultimate success. Nevertheless we need some success to maintain morale and to reassure us that we are on the right track. Thus the ideal racing programme should give rewarding results early in the season before we come to a peak for the more important races.

In Britain the racing calendar has evolved to present a wealth of opportunities just about every weekend throughout the year. Whether you are an ambitious competitor or racing just for fun you can use some of these races as an attractive way to help your development and give more obvious point to your training, and focus on one or two others as your major targets. As explained in Chapter 6 the periodization of the training year is a key concept, and your racing programme should be constructed to enhance the structure of your training and to raise the quality of your efforts. Thus what is needed is a series of head races through the autumn, winter and spring to encourage the long-term development of aerobic fitness, followed by shorter regatta racing to enhance speed and the techniques needed for the year's chief target events.

The majority of the long-distance head races in the autumn are for small boats including single sculls. I have already made the point that such small boats are the ideal vehicles in which to develop technique and to develop personal toughness, and I think that such races should be a regular part of the training schedule. Earlier I suggested that a two-week cycle between races might work best, as it allows both full recovery from the previous race and a long enough uninterrupted period of training in between. This might be too frequent if you taper the training significantly before each race, but some at least can be used as high quality training sessions without much interruption to your overall schedule, as shown in the earlier example of a training schedule for the St Edward's eight. Often the events offer separate divisions and different classes of boat throughout the day and I recommend that you take advantage of the opportunity.

The winter months have fewer events and in many years the weather and water conditions are less conducive to enjoyable racing. Training at this time is likely to be emphasizing strength and endurance development rather than speed, perhaps with a significant proportion being done on land, so it is probably best to do little or no racing at this time. The aim should be the very well patronized head races, some of very high status and standard indeed, which take place in March and April. The original Tideway Head of the River race was instituted as a way of encouraging clubs to do more endurance training in the winter, and has certainly succeeded in that objective. You should plan to take part and do your best in one or more of these big events as the culmination of your winter training. Some of the earlier heads can be fitted in to help develop your pace judgement, raise the quality of your training, or help to finalize crew selection.

For the summer regatta season a similar approach is needed, for we should sit down with a copy of the regatta timetable and pick out one or two competitive peaks, perhaps the National Schools Championships and Henley for example, and then work back from there. As before, a two-week cycle has advantages, but this may not fit with your other commitments or with the timing of regattas you really want to go to. If you are ambitious and aiming for the top with a real chance of success, then your aim will be to pick out the events that will give you the best preparation for the big ones that matter most. For others it will be more important to map out a series of well-run events that offer the right classes and are likely to attract worthy opponents. Either way you must take account of the need to spend some weeks in a transition period where you are learning to perform at higher ratings and speeds after the winter training and head season. You will also have to learn and rehearse the special techniques of regatta racing, such as the standing start and sprinting. You may not feel ready to race at all during this period, even if it could be useful practice, but prefer to make your debut when you are fully prepared.

To do all this you will require information both as to the past standard of the races, and also up-to-date information about the events offered. For the former you can look up last year's records of British domestic events in the indispensable *British Rowing Almanack*, or refer to the sometimes more extensive reports in back copies of the rowing magazines, as well as ask people who were there. Details of forthcoming events are published in the *Almanack* and in the magazines, and all clubs will be circulated with the necessary details. It is becoming increasingly common to be able to find what you want on appropriate websites.

REGATTA AND HEAD ORGANIZATION

Most events are run by groups of highly dedicated and very hard-working amateurs whose aim is to make their event as attractive and worthwhile as possible, and at the very least they deserve our co-operation. Standards and facilities vary enormously, from the slick tradition and precise attention to detail of Henley Royal Regatta, to the sort of informal event where entries and races change on the day. You may not be the person making the entry for the race in which you are going to compete, but you should be aware of the procedure and help to minimize any problems.

In general, every event will require full details of your entry and the fee at least a week in advance, and it is vital to check when the closing date falls. Online entries via BROE are made through the club administrator, and similar systems are in place with other federations

– it is usually possible to check that your entry has been safely received. If necessary you can notify changes of up to half of the crew not less than one hour before the event, but if this is not done properly you can be disqualified. If, as a result of crew changes or a win at an earlier regatta, your racing status changes, then the organizers may be able to fit you into an alternative event – and often a slot is set aside for just such an eventuality. Of course it is only prudent and courteous to warn the organizers of such changes, or a complete withdrawal, as far as possible in advance.

When you arrive at the venue (in very good time of course!), check in and complete any paperwork, pick up numbers and so on, and make a point of confirming that the timing and details of the event are exactly as you expect. Most organizers do try to stick to a precise timetable and it is very much in your interest and that of everyone else to help in this, so make sure that you boat and get to the start or marshalling area in good time. Some events have officials to chivvy you along, check who you are and that the cox is of the correct weight; others are a free-for-all and you will need to anticipate hold-ups as everyone tries to boat at the same time. For safety reasons there are usually regulations governing your route to the start, warm-up area and so on (see Chapter 4), and these can be very strictly enforced. As race time approaches, make sure that you are in the right place at the right time – don't paddle off for an extra bit of warm-up!

COMING TO A PEAK

As already mentioned, you may be using some events as part of your training and you may not wish to interrupt your schedule significantly. On the other hand there is no point in starting a race if you are still exhausted from previous training. In these cases it may only be necessary to ease your training for a day or two in order to perform well enough. However, the final weeks before a major competition should see considerable changes in your training pattern so that you are at your best at the time of the race. This is 'peaking' or 'tapering'. Just how much you have to modify your programme does of course depend on how much training you normally do, but for the purpose of this exercise let us assume that you have been training hard on a daily basis for some time. The supercompensation theory outlined in the previous chapter suggests that if you have been training hard you will not have fully recovered before the next training session, will be somewhat fatigued, and therefore not at your best.

In most cases it would be appropriate to start the 'taper' two weeks before the event you are aiming for by reducing the quantity of work in the first week but emphasizing the quality or speed. One week before the race there should be a day or two of more intense work related specifically to race pace and distance, and then a marked drop in quantity of work for the final week. In this last week there could be some useful pace or 'tempo' work three days before the race followed by two days of very light outings or rest. This system will give the best possible supercompensation on race day, maximize glycogen reserves (see Chapter 9), give good rehearsal of race pace and tactical bursts and leave you fresh and raring to go. Sometimes it can be difficult to convince yourself that that the reduction in training is wise, and inexperienced competitors often make the mistake of doing too much. Training hard in the last week is too late to do more than make you tired, your body will not have time to adapt, so if in doubt do less! Fig. 93 illustrates the pattern that training will take during the taper. This pattern will work for heads as well as for regattas, but of course the exact quantities and qualities will be very different for the two different types of event. The following schedule illustrates the more complex sort of training that a good club crew might undertake in peaking for a major regatta.

Fig. 93 Typical pattern of the quantity and quality of training when coming to a peak (tapering)

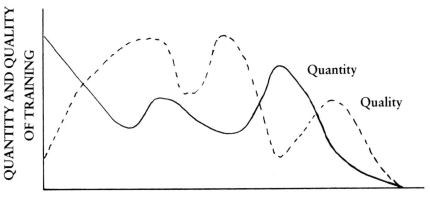

FINAL TWO WEEKS OF TRAINING

Training schedule for regatta peaking

Day	Training	Remarks
Saturday	Regatta	
Sunday	12 k steady state	Recover and technique
Monday	Stepped rating, 2 min each at rate 20, 22, 24, 26, 28, 26, 24, 22, 20	Endurance and technique
Tuesday	Fast fartlek pyramid, 10–40–10 strokes, 300 strokes total, practise starts	Developing speed
Wednesday	1 × 500 m, 2 × 1,000 m, 1 × 500 m, above race pace Time control	Speed endurance Pace judgement
Thursday	2(6×1min), 1½ min light paddling recovery	Speed endurance
Friday	Off	
Saturday	6 × 500 m, above race pace, 2½ min rest, 1st and last from standing start	Special endurance Pace judgement
Sunday	3 or 4 × 1,000 m, race pace, starts	Pace judgement
Monday	10 k steady state	Recovery and technique
Tuesday	2 or 3 × 5 min, below race pace	Recovery and technique
Wednesday	1 × 1,000 m, 1 × 500 m, starts	Pace judgement
Thursday	Light paddling, starts and sprints	Recovery and technique
Friday	Off	
Saturday	RACE	

RACE DAY PREPARATION

It seems to be a human characteristic that when we are preoccupied with some exciting happening, like going off to a race, we become forgetful – so it is wise to have a checklist. Are all the bits of boat, blades and spares, and the necessary tools, on the trailer or safely to hand? Do you have all your rowing kit? Do you have all the paperwork you might need? Food and drink? Do you and the rest of the crew know exactly where you are going and know exactly where and when you are to meet? How much time do you need to allow for a relaxing journey? Competition is necessarily stressful and it is very foolish to add to it with bad organization. Your need is to be calm and confident and have plenty of time to think about what you are doing. As explained in the next chapter, you should plan in advance what clothing you might need for the conditions on the day and your food and drink requirements. Correct nutrition and hydration is essential and possibly even more important for long-distance races than regattas. You may not sleep very well the night before, but that doesn't matter as long as you have been resting.

When you arrive your first priority is to make sure that the boat is ready and to ensure that the race is at the time you expect and has not been changed in any way. Don't waste energy by wandering around but sit somewhere warm if it is cold, or in the shade on a hot day. Make sure you have enough to drink, and think about when and what you are going to eat. As explained in the next chapter you should allow at least three hours for a full meal to digest and the last meal should be a light one of mostly carbohydrate and very little fat. You will probably find that nervousness reduces your appetite and may affect your digestion. As the time approaches to boat, sit quietly somewhere and go over your race tactics and options. Think what you intend to do and, in effect, mentally rehearse your race. Some people find that the right choice of music helps, and there is research evidence to back this. Do allow time to go to the toilet, and expect adrenalin to increase the frequency and urgency.

If you are racing again later in the day then your post-race imperatives are rest and hydration, probably some carbohydrate drink or energy gel, and food if you have time. Keep warm, remembering that a sweaty body can cool very rapidly. You may not need such an elaborate warm-up for the next race, but make sure that you have enough time for an adequate one. If you have finished for the day, rest and recuperation is still vital because what matters now is doing even better next time.

WARMING UP

An adequate warm-up is essential before a race not just because it literally warms up your muscles and readies your heart, lungs and other systems for the contest, but also because it helps you rehearse your

RACING 195

technique and gets you into the right frame of mind for the race. Often our pre-race nerves make us feel very weak, possibly even sick, and we wish we were somewhere else, as Matthew Pinsent has graphically described from his Olympic experiences. A good warm-up helps to overcome these qualms and replace them with concentration on the task in hand. In training you will have established a familiar pattern for your warm-up (as described in Chapter 6) and if you are able to follow much the same routine on race day it will be reassuring and of known efficacy. However, it is often the case that you will have to adopt a different plan, for example to fit in with marshalling for a head, or simply because of lack of space at a regatta. In any case most events have quite strict rules about proceeding to the start and warming up in the vicinity of the start. You should always find out about these limitations in advance and plan your revised warm-up accordingly. For example, if you know that you will be able to do little on the water you should have a more extensive land session before you boat.

A good warm-up for the first race will consist of your usual land procedure, say a ten minute jog and a range of mild stretching exercises, then boating as soon as possible and allowing about half an hour on the water before the start. The water work should be progressive; very easy technical exercises at first, gradually building into short bursts of firm pressure to increase heart and breathing rates and initiate sweating. At some events there is enough room to do a useful amount of work in race direction, and in some heads and multi-lane regattas you may be allowed onto the course (usually following a prescribed circulation pattern). It is very valuable to take advantage of this so that you can experience the race conditions and make the most realistic practice starts. Wear enough clothing to ensure that you do get warm, compatible with freedom of movement, and you should also have enough clothing with you to keep you warm if you have to wait for the start – the longest waits seem to be for heads in the middle of winter!

At regattas you will want to practise your racing start two or three times, and if you do about ten or fifteen strokes each time, flat out, this will release extra adrenalin but not too much lactic acid. You should finish these bursts a few minutes before you have to go onto the start, and wind down with a little light paddling. While waiting to be called on to the start you can busy yourself with final adjustments of clothing, checking gates, riggers and stretchers and perhaps having a last sip of drink. You must be at, or attached to, the start and ready to race at

Fig. 94 Preparing for the start. The crew is nervous but ignoring their opponents and concentrating on what they have to do

least two minutes before race time, and it is important to arrange things so that you are neither late and flustered nor left sitting around with nothing to do except worry. Don't watch your opponents but concentrate on your own boat and what you have to do.

REGATTA RACING – THE RACING START

For tactical reasons it is very important to be able to move off the start very cleanly and quickly and to settle into your chosen race rhythm well. If you develop a good starting procedure it will give you a much greater choice of tactics and boost your confidence, even if you choose to go off with something in hand. Technically the start presents some special problems because you will be applying greater than usual force to a boat which at first is not moving, and then accelerates rapidly to a much higher than usual speed, while you row or scull at a much higher than usual rating.

Let us take first the simplest case of a stake-boat or fixed start on still water. You will have backed carefully onto the start and will be held by the person there. They have little to hold on to, and if it is your rudder you don't want it damaged, so when you are trying to get the boat straight do not wrench it away. Backing down on one side as you paddle-on with the other will turn you in place.

Remember that to move the bows round or to counteract a cross-wind, it is much more effective to slide forward and take just the beginning of the stroke. If there is a strong cross-wind, or you are badly out of line, then it may be necessary for someone in the bows to give their blade to the person in front so that they can pull the boat round with the blade almost parallel with the side, a move that you should have rehearsed in training. In such a wind it is a good idea to keep your boat heading into the wind because it is much easier to hold it there. If you judge it well you can then let the boat swing round just before the start so it is pointing the right way at the exact moment.

Listen to the starter and make sure that he or she knows if you are not ready. This is usually done by cox or bow (or both) raising their hands, though in a single you may have your hands full and will have to shout. A good starter will see that you are not ready, but do not rely on it, and try to keep straight and ready when you are attached. Sometimes the starter will tell you how the start will be carried out but it is always worth watching previous races to be sure. Usually there will be someone checking that the boats are aligned and then the starter will tell anyone who has been given an 'official warning' (say for being late on the start) which means disqualification if they then 'false start', i.e. cross the line before the 'Go!' The starter should then call out the race number, event and possible outcome (e.g. 'first crew to final') before carrying out the 'roll call', naming each crew or sculler in turn. After the roll call the start could be at any time and the starter does not have to respond if you are not ready – indeed, the starter can tell you to put your hand down if it is delaying the start. The starter then says 'Attention!', raises a red flag, and then lowers it as the word 'Go!' is given. There is a variable pause between the two words. On international standard courses there will be other devices such as coloured lights or flags to indicate the 'Attention' and the 'Go', together with an audible signal, and perhaps even a clamp to hold the bows straight. It is essential to familiarize yourself with the system before your race.

On still water I advise that the blades are already squared and covered in the water and that you are sitting ready before the start is called. Otherwise, you will lose a fraction of a second and a last-moment squaring and covering of the blade can upset the boat and can cause mistakes. With stake-boats on a slow-moving river (Henley for example) the same procedure will apply, but if there is a fast stream

Fig. 95 Good body and blade
positions ready for the start

you will have to modify your approach. If the flow is in race direction
you can either keep the blades out of the water until the 'Go' or turn
them slightly over-square. Either way, you must practise the procedure
because it is easy to lose control and the pressure on the blade will be
much greater than usual – indeed, it might be worth shortening your
first stroke so that you can get it through quickly. When the water is
flowing against you it is more difficult to keep the boat straight and
more difficult to grip the water on the first stroke, so it may be best to
delay squaring and covering the blades and worth taking a longer first
stroke. If it is a free start the problems may be less but you need to
make sure that you are in the right position and not moving backwards
before the start.

The starting procedure that I favour begins with a quite long first
stroke using most of the slide, but keeping the heels down, and little
forward lean of the body. The object is to accelerate the boat very
hard but smoothly, but in fact it does not move very far in that first
stroke, nor does it begin to move the instant you start pulling but may
even go backwards. Every member of the crew must start with his or
her blades in the same relative position, and the sculler must have the

blades symmetrically placed. Drive very hard with the legs and hold the back very firm in order to transmit this great force to the stationary boat without 'bum-shoving'. The blades must be better covered in the water than usual to stop them slipping and this good coverage of the blades must be continued to the finish so that they do not wash out. In a sculling boat it can be helpful to reach out a little further and apply a little pressure as a gentle squeeze just before the start. This takes up any slack and ensures that the sculls are properly squared and locked in the water. Good timing and balance is crucial for the slow-moving boat must be level for the next stroke, so make sure that all blades leave the water together. Never cut this finish short but do get the hands away extra smartly.

The second stroke should be taken very quickly, so quickly that it is shorter than the first. Timing this is not easy and will require a lot of practice. This short, quick, driving stroke builds on the momentum of the first stroke, and by moving forwards quickly for it you actually help to accelerate the boat. The third stroke should also be taken very quickly, but should be a longer one. And now that the boat is really beginning to shift, the catches and finishes will need to be very fast and clean. Because of the extra power and bigger puddles, it is necessary to exaggerate the actions at the finish to make sure that the blades do not wash out yet clear the water. The fourth and fifth strokes will be virtually full length but very fast and powerful because the boat is already moving fast yet must still accelerate. It may take ten strokes to get the boat up to full speed and for tactical reasons you may continue much further at the higher speed.

A full-blooded racing start is very exhilarating but also uses up a great deal of energy. Fortunately reserves of anaerobic power are available when you are fresh, but these soon run out and to continue at maximum speed will demand more anaerobic work that will create lactic acid. Exactly where you 'stride' into a more economical rhythm depends on your choice of tactics and you can do it by a gradual lengthening and steadying of the strokes, or more abruptly at a pre-arranged signal. The danger is that as the excitement of the start passes you may fall to too low a pace, and this often coincides with feeling of breathlessness and weakness as your body struggles to adjust to the race. It is vital to convince yourself that this is just a passing feeling and that you must push very hard into the race proper, and of course you must have rehearsed this difficult phase very thoroughly in training.

Fig. 96 The start – first stroke. A lot of power is being applied against very well covered blades. The boats have not yet moved!

Fig. 97 The start – on to the second stroke. Clean finishes to the first stroke enable the second to be taken very quickly using only a fraction of the slide. Note that the blades are taken high on the feather to clear the puddles

Fig. 98 The start – third stroke. Taken quickly but with more slide and already the near crew is ahead

RACE PROFILES

An experienced competitor's effort is distributed in a characteristic way over the race distance, and the overall pattern is much the same for all boat types but does differ significantly between different race distances. Within this broad pattern there are usually important variations according to the abilities of, or tactics adopted by, the crews or scullers in a particular race. These adjustments of pace within the overall profile of the race can be of crucial importance, and can have an effect on the athletes that might be surprising at first.

As was discussed in earlier chapters it is important to bear in mind, firstly the way in which resistance is related to boat speed, and secondly the metabolic cost of increased power. It is a fundamental of hydrodynamics that resistance increases approximately as the velocity squared, and that the power required will then increase by the cube of the speed increase. Thus any small increase in speed, say for tactical reasons, will require a large increase in power. In a hard race the athlete is already functioning very close to the limit of his or her capabilities, and in particular probably above the maximum aerobic energy production (known as the anaerobic threshold). Thus an increase in power over and above this will cause a sharp rise in anaerobic energy production, with a particularly large rise in harmful waste products (see again fig. 83 in Chapter 7). On the other hand we have already seen from Chapters 6 and 7 that reserves of power are available in the short term both in the early stages of the race and in the final minute (see again fig. 75 in Chapter 6). Thus the best race profile may not be exactly even paced, even if we neglect the possible psychological advantages of a fast start or tactical surges.

Head races

Head races are usually longer than regatta courses and because you are not racing side by side the tactical considerations will be very different. The aim is to cover the course as quickly as possible at the optimum even pace, because this is the most efficient use of energy. This means that you do not carry out a racing start and you avoid any marked changes in the pace until perhaps a minute or two before the finish. Even so you will have some extra energy at the beginning of the race, and you might choose to go off at a higher speed for the first minute or so in order to

Fig. 99 Overtaking in a head race can be a problem even though the slower crews should move out of the way

maintain position with your rivals. It may even help you to settle into a good pace if you set off a bit faster and then stretch out to your race pace, and it is worth experimenting with this in training. Sometimes too it can be worthwhile increasing your speed a little as you come up to overtake a significant rival, so as to make the move incisive and perhaps morale-boosting. You may also wish to get past quickly to resume a better course on the river. The key thing to remember is that even pace is not even effort – as you tire it will seem harder and harder to maintain. I recommend that you try out the strategy on the ergometer and I think you will find that something close to even pace works best.

Regatta races

As an example of a classic front running race profile let us take the case of the victory of Redgrave and Holmes in the coxless pair at the Seoul Olympics. Characteristically Redgrave dictated the pace from start to finish, and it was these tactics which brought him his greatest successes and of course enhanced his aura of invincibility. If we analyse their race profile (fig. 100) we see that not only does the boat's speed change in a characteristic manner but that the way in which the pair achieves and maintains that speed also changes substantially during the race. As a consequence the technical requirements of the different sectors also vary, as do the physiological demands on the athletes. A rowing race

	500 m	1,000 m	1,500 m	2,000 m
Cumulative times	1.34.9	3.15.4	4.57.3	6.36.8
Split times		1.40.5	1.41.9	1.39.5

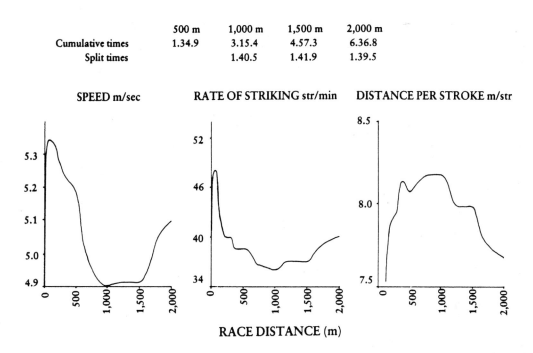

SPEED m/sec   RATE OF STRIKING str/min   DISTANCE PER STROKE m/str

RACE DISTANCE (m)

Fig. 100 Video analysis of the race profile of the Great Britain 2–, Olympic Games, 1988

(even over the so-called sprint distance of 500 metres) is not a simple flat-out effort; rather it is a subtle and finely judged blend of physical and physiological capacity matched to the tactical requirements of the race. Let us now analyse the sectors of the race in more detail.

1 The start

A fast and effective start is essential in side-by-side racing, partly for psychological reasons but also to prevent the opponents gaining any critical advantage. As we have seen, the start requires special and very well rehearsed technique, the application of great amounts of power, and a very high stroke frequency. The energy cost is very high but at this point in the race reserves of power are available that will not be there later in the race and the nervous and muscular systems are at peak efficiency. Both the video and the split times show that the British pair started very fast, but this is what they had trained for. They were capable of speeds at this stage of the race that would have been suicidal for their rivals.

2 Transition to race pace and establishing a position

In a 2,000-metre race it is usual for the pace to be particularly fast during the first 300–600 metres until the crew or sculler changes from the initial charge off the start to the power and rhythm that can be sustained for the bulk of the race. At the same time tactical considerations will be much in evidence as the boats jockey for position. In this Olympic final, Redgrave and Holmes had established an early lead and were thus best placed to judge exactly what they must do to maintain it. Rates of striking are still higher than in the middle sector of the race and despite the higher boat speed, the distance covered per stroke is less. This is not because the length of stroke in the water is necessarily shorter (indeed at this stage the athletes are trying to lengthen it), but rather because the rapid rhythm does not allow the boat to run so far before the next catch.

3 The cruise

In this sector, often the middle 1,000 metres of a 2,000-metre race, the competitor's target is to achieve or maintain the chosen tactical position with the minimum expenditure of energy. It is necessary therefore to establish a pace of the greatest physiological efficiency, that is, where the energy output is matched almost entirely by aerobic energy production (see again fig. 75). Good technique is vitally important in husbanding resources, and as shown in fig. 100 the rate of striking will be minimized whilst the distance travelled per stroke will be maximized. The winners are likely to be those who arrive at the end of this sector in a good tactical position and with the greatest physical resources in hand.

If we look again at fig. 100, we see that at about 1,100 metres into the race the British pair increase their speed, and this was in response to a challenge from their nearest rivals. It is clear from this that the pair had something in hand and were determined to use it to maintain their lead throughout, and not leave anything to chance in the last stage of the race.

4 The final spurt

It is common for the work rate to begin to rise at about 500 metres from home in a 2,000-metre race, with more dramatic increases in the last 45–60 seconds. As fig. 100 shows, the rate increases and the distance per stroke falls. Although the athletes are summoning every last bit of their resources, the boat speed does not increase by all that much because both power and technical skills are fading owing to increasing fatigue. The power produced aerobically will be declining as the waste products accumulate, but the final anaerobic reserves are now being called upon. The waste products will soon bring effective muscle contraction to a halt – but it is the end of the race.

Winning from the front like this is very satisfying but does not suit every athlete. To take the British crews at the Sydney Olympics as an example, the coxless four with Redgrave on board again took an early lead and showed that no one was going to get past them. The eight used the same tactic, and when I asked Steve Trapmore, the stroke, if he had been at all anxious about leading an Olympic final by nearly a length at halfway, he said no – it was what they had planned. Now there is confidence in your training and tactics! For the coxless pair however, their early lead took too much out of them and they were unable to match the fast finishes of three other crews – most notably the French who had husbanded their resources and produced a stunning burst of speed for the final 500 metres to take the gold.

RACE TACTICS

The balance between available energy and speed over the course is a very delicate one and the wrong choice can be disastrous. Psychologically the chosen tactics and the way they unfold between competitors during the race can make a crucial difference to the individual performances. Some will be lifted by the success of their tactical responses or pre-planned

Fig. 101 A clean and effective start by the GB Junior women's four in Munich gives the crew an immediate advantage and a choice of tactics

moves and their perception of fatigue will be altered, whilst others will be demoralized by their apparent failure or by their rivals' surprise moves. It is at such times that our mental strength is tested, and also when a well-informed and canny cox can be a major asset.

To illustrate a range of tactics used in a high-quality race I have chosen the very exciting and closely fought final of the coxless fours in the Junior World Championships of 1988. The times for the six crews are given in Table 12.

Table 12

Coxless four final, Junior Men 1988, cumulative times and position (in brackets), split times, and deficit on leader at 500-metre intervals

Crew	Finish position	500 m	1,000 m	1,500 m
Italy	1	1.27.09 (4) 1.32–	3.00.33 (5) 1.33.24 4.29–	4.27.69 (1) 1.27.36
France	2	1.25.77 (1) 0.25–	2.56.29 (2) 1.30.52	4.28.34 (2) 1.32.05 0.65–
Great Britain	3	1.28.45 (6) 2.68–	2.59.50 (4) 1.31.05 3.46–	4.28.71 (3) 1.29.21 1.02–
East Germany	4	1.26.41 (3) 0.64–	2.57.91 (3) 1.31.50 1.87–	4.30.51 (4) 1.32.60 2.82–
Czechoslovakia	5	1.25.97 (2) 0.20–	2.56.04 (1) 1.30.07	4.30.93 (5) 1.34.89 3.24–
Soviet Union	6	1.27.63 (5) 1.86–	3.00.60 (6) 1.32.97 4.56–	4.33.22 (6) 1.32.62 5.53–

The three medallists (Italy, France and Britain) show three very different but common strategies. The Italian crew, perhaps confident of their fast finish, set off at moderate speed, content not to lead in the early stages but to remain well in touch. Their speed stayed steady in the first part of the course as they saved themselves and gathered for

Fig. 102 The final moments of the epic Junior World Championships in coxless fours. The Italians (nearest the camera) are moving into the lead as the GB four next to them overhaul the Czech crew in lane 5 but just fail to catch the French (lane 6)

their most effective final run for the line. The French gambled on a very fast start and opening pace, as did the Czechoslovakian crew, which they maintained as long as possible. Such tactics can have two benefits in that an unassailable lead might be built up before the more cautious respond, and sometimes the opposition may be rattled by this early demonstration of greater speed. The penalty, as both crews demonstrate, is the metabolic cost of such a fast early pace and the inevitable slowing towards the end. In this case the gamble nearly paid off for the French, as the Czechs, who had gone even harder for the lead at halfway, could not hold on. The British crew intended to race more evenly, believing that to be most efficient and knowing that they had the ability to achieve a strong finish. In the event they may have wished to have been higher placed after the start, and therefore with less to do to move up in the middle of the race. But it is probable that they used their resources most effectively and completely but could not match the Italians' final surge.

The best competitors will understand these principles and will have developed and thoroughly rehearsed their ideal race plan. They will also have the flexibility to adopt another if the circumstances require, and the ability to respond as necessary to the tactics of their opponents.

In multi-lane racing or in an event with a *repêchage* system (second chance to qualify), you may not need to win your heat in order to progress to the next round. It is of course essential to check very carefully what the rules are, and to work out what all the implications of finishing in any position will be when it comes to later rounds. There are psychological attractions in finishing first and in many cases the

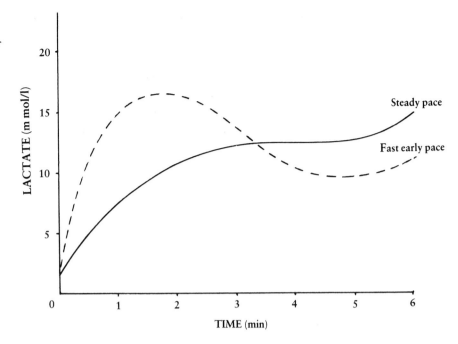

Fig. 103 Lactate production in a race depends on the pace – too much early on will hamper later efforts

event is organized in such a way that the winners get the easiest passage to the final or perhaps the best lanes. On the other hand there is no point in racing flat out if you don't benefit from it. The best plan is usually to race hard for the first part of the course and then assess what needs to be done. If possible at least avoid a sprint finish and its lactic acid and save yourself for the races that matter more.

THE UMPIRE

The umpires are there to help you and to ensure that racing is fair and carried out according to the rules and regulations. These do change from time to time and you must be aware of the ones in force. At the start an aligner or the starter will be watching for false starts, that is, if your bows cross the line before the flag falls. In the event of a false start, or if something is wrong, then a red flag will be waved and a bell rung to halt the race. There will be a restart and the offender will be awarded one false start penalty – if they offend again they will be disqualified.

During the race the umpire may follow in a launch, along the bank on a bicycle, or be stationed at intervals on the bank. Their main task is to ensure that each competitor stays on their proper course and does not interfere with their opponents; errors can be punished by disqualification even though you may be well ahead at the time. If the umpires see that you are going astray they should warn you and indicate what you must do. If they tell you to move to 'Port' or 'Starboard' you should know what it means and respond promptly. If all goes well the umpire at the finish will raise a white flag to show the judges that there are no problems, but if there was a problem then a red flag means that umpire and officials must confer and make a decision. If you are unhappy about the race and wish to protest, then draw the umpire's attention before the white flag is raised and express (politely!) your grievance.

THE DRUG PROBLEM

My own attitude to anyone who deliberately takes any artificial substance to boost their performance either in training or racing is simply stated: they are cheating. To my mind any success gained that way is not worth having, and I am fully in favour of strong measures to detect abuse, punish offenders, and deter those who might consider it. Furthermore, many of the substances that could be used in an attempt to improve performance are harmful. Although we now know that there was some systematic cheating in some countries in the past, our sport has been relatively free of problems in recent years. This is probably because the financial rewards are not great, there are few drugs of known efficacy, and because rowers and scullers have been subject to random testing of increasing sophistication for some years.

The World Anti-Doping Agency (WADA) and its Medical Commission, together with the governing bodies of the various sports and their medical advisers, issue up-to-date guidelines and a list of banned substances. FISA, the governing body of our sport, adopts the WADA list almost in its entirety. Essentially the list specifies a large number of substances which must not be found in the competitor's body at the time of competition, those which may be permitted providing they have medical clearance well in advance (such as some asthma drugs), and those which must not be found during the training period. This leaves the doctors free to use a wider range of treatments and medicines for genuine illness during training. Information on all of this is available from the governing bodies in each country and in Britain this would be BR or its International Rowing Office.

You are held entirely responsible for anything untoward that is found in your system whatever its origin – ignorance is no excuse. There are some problems that occur that you must be aware of and avoid. Many proprietary medicines that are freely available at pharmacies contain banned substances, and these particularly include painkillers and treatments for the symptoms of coughs and colds. You may be prescribed drugs for some other condition which unknown to you might contain a forbidden substance. You should discuss this with your doctor and make sure there is no problem. There are many examples of athletes in other sports who have had problems with dietary supplements (which probably don't work anyway) which contained something illegal, apparently unknown to them. A high proportion of such supplements does contain banned substances (including the ones supplied to tennis players by their own federation!) and these are not shown on the label. Many herbal preparations are far from pure and you are unlikely to know what is in them. Take nothing that you are not certain about. And finally, 'recreational' drugs are also very likely to be a problem even weeks later.

Science advances very rapidly and the cheats become more sophisticated in their attempts to keep ahead of the testing. All of us in sport must be quick to condemn such abuses and strong in our support for the authorities battling against them.

9 Looking After Yourself

A competitor in a demanding sport such as ours must not only train to get the utmost return for the effort put in, but must also try hard to ensure that there are no adverse and avoidable influences hampering performance. Good health is essential and to be really successful you must be determined to avoid the insults to health that so many of the population allow themselves – smoking, poor diet, excess alcohol, bad hygiene, and so on. Our environment may not be optimal either, yet many of the problems it may pose are easily minimized. A further problem is that most of us pick up all sorts of ideas about health and diet, which may or may not be true or helpful. For example I would be prepared to bet that some readers believe that a big steak the night before is the ideal preparation for a race, or that after training in hot weather they need to take salt tablets. The purpose of this chapter, then, is to give you a working guide to the maintenance of the athletic body, and partly to dispel some unhelpful myths.

ENVIRONMENTAL CONDITIONS

Because rowing is an outdoor sport it is essential for you to know how to cope with and adapt to a wide range of environmental conditions. Poor preparation in this case can have results ranging from discomfort to death, and the problems must therefore be taken very seriously. For the athlete the result of inadequate preparation or adaptation can also be a disastrously poor performance. Fortunately our bodies do adapt considerably even to quite extreme conditions given time and careful planning, and we can minimize the problems with intelligent foresight.

There are four major categories of environmental stress, which need to be considered, namely heat, cold, air pollution and altitude. Other factors such as wind or humidity can interact with these and will also be considered in this chapter.

Heat

At maximal effort the rower or sculler will generate something in the order of 5.0 megajoules (MJ) of heat per hour – that would be enough to raise the temperature of the 40 litres or so of water in the body by 2.8° C in a six-minute race. To this heat may be added radiant heat from the sun, and convection from a hot atmosphere if its temperature exceeds that of the skin (about 32° C). The normal mean body temperature is 36.7° C and stabilizing mechanisms, controlled by the hypothalamus of the brain, respond to small changes in both core and skin temperatures by changing metabolic rate, skin blood vessel dilation and sweating.

Even in a cool climate the main way in which heat is lost during vigorous exercise is by the evaporation of sweat, when the energy for the evaporation is taken from the skin and indirectly from the blood supplying it. One litre of sweat removes 2.43 MJ of heat, thus to lose the athlete's extra heat production of 5.0 MJ/hr would require the evaporation of more than two litres per hour. The rate of evaporation is increased considerably by wind, and the movement of the boat will help even though only bow gets the full benefit! Humidity reduces the rate of evaporation and the worst combination will be a still, sunny day, with both high humidity and high air temperature. Even in low relative humidity, more than 50% of the total sweat will run off the body, with little cooling effect, rather than evaporate.

Intensive exercise produces so much heat so quickly that although these cooling systems are activated the core temperature still rises. A rise to about 38° C would have no adverse effects, and in fact helps to increase the rate of heat loss and speed up metabolic processes. Muscles become less viscous and can contract faster, joints move more easily, and the circulation is also helped. These are the beneficial thermal effects of the warm-up. Trained athletes working very hard can experience even greater rises – to 40° C or more – and can tolerate such rises without harm if they are brief. However, longer periods or higher temperatures can be very dangerous.

Three major problems can arise:

1   *Heat exhaustion.*   The effects of heat include a higher heart rate for any given level of effort, a reduction in VO_2 max., poorer endurance, a lower anaerobic threshold, and, if dehydration occurs, a reduced heart stroke volume and reduced circulation to the muscles. Obviously performance is reduced. The greater danger comes from dehydration brought about by the inevitable high sweat rate, which could then lead to more serious heat illness. Treatment should consist of sipping cold water or dilute drinks (see later), and cooling the skin by sponging and fanning.

2   *Heat collapse.*   The collapse is due to poor blood flow to the brain and is most likely after a race or hard training session when a lot of blood has been diverted to the skin for cooling, and then there is a pooling of blood in the muscles when the cessation of activity reduces blood return through the veins and so starves the brain of its essential supplies. Standing will make the situation worse (fig. 104), so lying supine with the legs elevated will help, as will cooling and drinks as before. If the core temperature is above 41° C then heat stroke should be suspected.

Fig. 104 The GB Junior eight receiving their medals in Zagreb – one member of the crew is close to collapse and a chair has been provided

3   *Heat stroke.*   Prolonged or extreme overheating can lead to a failure of the body's heat regulating mechanisms. This is potentially fatal and requires urgent medical treatment and hospitalization. Symptoms may include excessive sweating or failure of sweating, headache, dizziness, nausea, convulsions and disturbances of consciousness. Emergency treatment requires gradual body cooling.

Dehydration

Although less dramatic than the illnesses listed above, the long-term losses of water and minerals in sweat during hot weather are performance limiting and potentially dangerous. As we have seen the losses when working hard can be well in excess of 2 l/hr, which is 2.9% of the body weight of a 70 kg athlete. Losses of 2% will certainly reduce performance significantly, increasing core temperature and the heart rate still more, and tending to cause irritability and lowered motivation to work. It has been estimated that each 1% loss of body fluid reduces performance by 2–5%. More will be said about fluid replacement later in the chapter, but it is important to appreciate that water can only be absorbed at a rate of 600–700 ml/hr. It follows that rapid oral rehydration is not possible, even if a lot of water is drunk rapidly, and that you will be unable to maintain fluid levels during prolonged training in hot weather despite regular intake of drinks. You must become used to drinking small amounts at frequent intervals so that your body starts each training session or competition as fully hydrated as possible and is replenished as rapidly as possible.

Sweat contains many salts (electrolytes) which are essential to the body, and losses of sodium chloride for example may reach 8 g/hr. If we have good reserves then the amounts in the blood plasma actually rise during exercise, so in the short term we don't have to add to them *during* exercise, but we do have to replace them afterwards and perhaps in long training sessions or very long races as well. If cumulative losses are great then you are liable to feel tired and irritable and may suffer giddiness, cramps and perhaps falls in blood pressure. Replenishment is easy through electrolyte drinks or just through the normal diet, but salt tablets are much too concentrated and may not be absorbed or may even lead to the kidneys excreting extra salt.

Training and racing in hot weather

The well-trained athlete will already have some heat tolerance but this will increase considerably after about a week in a hotter climate. This adjustment is termed acclimatization. There will be increases in blood pressure and blood volume which help to cover the larger flow through the skin, and there will be a major change in sweating. After acclimatization sweating will start earlier in the exercise and will be greater in volume, whilst its salt content will be reduced. As a result of the changes you will not only perform better but will also feel more comfortable. If you know that you will have to race or train in hot conditions then protective preparation must be undertaken.

Experience of working in heat is important and outings could be moved to a hotter time of day or you could wear more clothing. This will help; but is not as effective as a naturally hot environment. Ideally you should have a week or more to acclimatize at the race venue, and at least one outing a day at race time. Allowance must be made for the enervating effect of the heat so that excessive fatigue is not experienced. As mentioned earlier, you must be in the habit of drinking frequently and should always have your own drink bottle in the boat – never share because of the risk of infection. Drinking only when thirsty is too late, for by then you have lost a significant amount of fluid – the best guide is that your urine is copious and pale, for then you can be sure that you have been drinking enough. Great attention must be paid to recovery between training sessions with yet more fluid and good nutrition. Avoid alcoholic drinks because they are diuretic (cause the kidneys to excrete more water).

Lightweight, loose-fitting clothing will minimize the effects of the sun and allow sweat to evaporate. Traditionally, cotton was recommended but it retains sweat and becomes uncomfortable and there are now several synthetics (not nylon) which help sweat to wick away from the skin and evaporate. Wet hair and clothing can help cooling but the athlete must beware of the likely contamination of the water in most courses and avoid using it for this purpose. Even mild sunburn reduces performance and any exposed skin should be covered with a high-protection factor sunscreen. Some people find hats useful while others regard them as oppressive and uncomfortable. Sunglasses reduce the glare from the water, which can otherwise prove tiring and may be harmful.

Fig. 105 Lycra can be combined with a number of other fibres to make rowing suits that fit well and are comfortable in action even when wet

On a hot race day it is important that you should stay in the shade before racing, preferably where there is a breeze, and should use a minimal-length, but tested and effective, warm-up when you go on the water. It is wise to time the end of the warm-up to give just a few minutes' calm before the start, but to avoid sitting motionless and frying in the sun! At the end of the race try to arrange a decent wind-down to avoid the problems of a sudden fall in blood pressure, and start to drink straight away.

There is a common fallacy that training in layers of thick clothing to induce copious sweating in some way speeds up gains in fitness, or helps in losing fat. Maybe this arises from pictures of boxers trying to make the weight. Apart from any danger of overheating it should be obvious that this strategy will reduce performance, endurance and training capacity, and therefore will in fact reduce fitness gains and fat losses. Lightweights must be very wary of trying to lose weight through dehydration – a temporary loss of up to a kilo may not matter but larger or longer-term losses do.

Cold

Rowers or scullers face several possible categories of problems if they train or race in cold weather, particularly if it is also wet and windy – for wet clothes have little insulation value and wind causes much more rapid evaporative cooling (the wind chill factor). Although fit athletes are capable of generating a great deal of heat they are also more at risk because of their lower percentage of insulating body fat. Particular thought must also be given to the special hazards for the relatively immobile coxswain. The problems that you are most likely to encounter in training and racing are these:

1 *Lower than optimum core temperatures* Even a one-degree fall will significantly impair performance. The speed of muscle contraction is slowed and the greater viscosity will increase effort. The relaxation of antagonistic muscles is also slowed and this makes co-ordination more difficult. Energy supplies will be depleted more rapidly than usual by the extra demands of heat generation. If you are so cold that you are shivering then the outing should probably be abandoned. If you grip the handle too tightly you will restrict the circulation in your fingers, which will then lose sensation as they become too cold, and then very painful as they warm up later.

2 *Hypothermia* Exhaustion and collapse can occur because of rapid falls in blood sugar but low body temperatures themselves can bring about loss of consciousness. 35° C is the critical low temperature below which mental confusion and poor muscle control precede a loss of control of body temperature that is potentially fatal. Food, sugary hot drinks, and warm clothing or blankets can bring rapid recovery. Coaching launches should always carry survival blankets.

3 *Frostbite* In severe cold the withdrawal of blood from the extremities can lead to actual freezing of the exposed tissues such as fingers, nose and ears. A white, waxy appearance and numbness are symptoms to be taken seriously and demand immediate re-warming of the afflicted parts.

4 *Falling into cold water* Survival time may be only 15 minutes in cold water close to freezing, as heat loss and the onset of hypothermia will be rapid. Sudden immersion in cold water causes gasping and possible inhalation of water – it can also be difficult to hold the breath long enough to escape from an overturned boat. In

addition, especially if the shock of immersion comes to a warm athlete whose circulatory system is in full flow, there may be harmful disturbances to the heart's rhythm. Rescue and rapid re-warming of the victim must always be first priority and all coaching launches must be suitably equipped.

Training and racing in cold weather

Acclimatization to cold is less obvious than to heat, but greater heat production and reduced blood flow to the skin will make you feel more comfortable and better able to deal with the cold. Careful choice of clothing is the obvious key to maintaining safety and performance in the cold but it requires matching freedom of movement with adequate insulation. As a general principle it is best to use the multiple thin layers of clothing since this will trap more air for insulation and will enable layers to be shed as you warm up. Synthetic thermal wear is ideal since it is light, stretchy, fits snugly and does not retain moisture. The outer layer should be waterproof and windproof but breathable, for sweaty insulation is not much good. A hat and gloves, at least while warming up or when waiting, are also a good idea. The same principles apply to the cox, who can pay even more attention to the waterproofing of the kit and can usefully have even better insulation. A

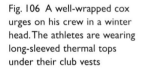

Fig. 106 A well-wrapped cox urges on his crew in a winter head. The athletes are wearing long-sleeved thermal tops under their club vests

coxswain's feet can get very cold but heavy shoes must be avoided for safety reasons.

Particular thought should be given to the warm-up. A vigorous session in the boathouse will raise internal temperature and establish good circulation before going on the water. Less clothing can be worn for this so that it does not get wet with perspiration and lose its insulation value, but more layers will be needed outside to prevent rapid chilling of the now warm body surface. You should try to boat and get into action as quickly as possible, and interruptions should be minimized. In some competitions, and that means most heads, a wait before the start is inevitable and it is wise to carry extra clothing in a polythene bag – the extra weight is less harmful to performance than a cold athlete! When you finish you need to put on adequate clothing, for you will cool down very rapidly.

Air pollution

Burning fossil carbon fuels releases many gases that are harmful to health and athletic performance. Although mainly a problem of urban areas many of us have to train on waterways in such locations and will probably also run through the streets as part of our land training. Some forms of smog tend to accumulate in low-lying areas where many of our rowing clubs are found. Some of the commonest pollutants increase the risk of infections such as bronchitis, reduce airflow to the lungs and will cause problems for asthmatics at very low concentrations. Dangerous concentrations are frequently found in our city streets, particularly during rush hour and in the winter. Another serious pollutant is the carbon monoxide from vehicle exhausts – which has the highly undesirable effect of combining with haemoglobin to form carboxyhaemoglobin. This will effectively prevent that haemoglobin from transporting oxygen until the monoxide has been eliminated, and it takes 3–4 hours to get rid of half of it. Levels of 35 parts per million are harmful and 100 ppm is often exceeded on city streets and levels above 500 ppm have been recorded in underpasses and tunnels.

Clearly the best advice is to avoid congested areas and not train in foggy conditions or if there are specific smog or air quality warnings. It would be wise to bear the problem in mind if you are travelling through a polluted area to train or race.

If you are interested enough in health and fitness to be reading this book then you probably don't smoke. Anyone who does should be aware that tobacco smoke contains carbon monoxide (putting 10% of the smoker's haemoglobin out of action), nicotine and a large range of carcinogens. The smoke will have a directly harmful effect on the airways and longer-term effects that will predispose towards lung disease – only 2% of chronic bronchitis sufferers are non-smokers who live in rural areas. Nicotine and other substances in tobacco tar damage the circulatory system in both the short and long term. There is no question that the athletic performance of a smoker is seriously compromised.

Altitude

The 1968 Olympics in Mexico City provoked a great deal of interest in both the problems of competing at altitude and the possible advantages of training there. The reduction in air density with altitude lowers wind resistance so that times for short distances (say 500 metres) will be reduced, but since there will be a corresponding reduction in oxygen partial pressure, aerobic capacity will be much less. In Mexico City (2,240 metres) the air pressure (and oxygen) is about 24% lower than at sea level, and performances in the 1968 Olympic Regatta were about 5–8% down on what might have been expected at sea level. Additional problems include increased UV radiation and sunburn and the lower carbon dioxide partial pressures which can disturb the normal breathing control mechanisms. Medical problems such as pulmonary oedema (fluid in the lungs) and possible heart problems may occur when exercise is undertaken at altitude, and the risk is more severe above 2,500 metres.

Acclimatization

Some people do not acclimatize well to altitude, but those who do will experience a number of physiological changes that enable them to perform better at altitude. The changes occur particularly during the first 1–2 weeks but some continue to accumulate over a longer period – but there is always an advantage to those who normally live at height. Some of the early adjustments will temporarily reduce performance even more, and others will be a hindrance when the athlete returns to sea level.

On first arrival at altitude there is a tendency to hyperventilate to meet the body's oxygen requirement, but most people quickly settle to a more normal rhythm. The low carbon dioxide level, which is made worse by hyperventilation, disturbs the breathing control mechanism. During the first week, progressive loss of buffers from the blood normally occurs so that breathing becomes more normal and some of the oxygen deficit can be made up. Also during the first week there is a loss in plasma volume that effectively concentrates the blood and improves oxygen transport. The reduction in volume continues during the next few weeks and consequently the blood thickens, which may hamper free circulation. Maximum heart output may be reduced and VO_2 max. depressed. Both the rate of destruction and the rate of production of red blood cells will increase, and it is normal to experience a rise in both red cell count and haemoglobin (fig. 107), although this will further increase the blood's viscosity.

Training at altitude can be used as a stimulus to increase the enzymes responsible for aerobic respiration in muscle, to increase the number of capillaries and to increase levels of myoglobin, the oxygen transfer substance in muscle. Obviously, anaerobic respiration will set

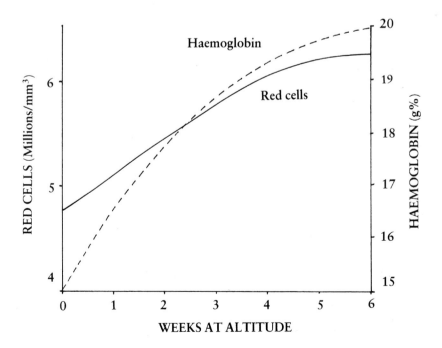

Fig. 107 Red cell numbers and the haemoglobin they carry both increase rapidly during the first weeks at altitude

in at lower work levels and lactate production will rise earlier than at sea level. This could be a problem with the lowered buffering capacity that develops, but fortunately the enzymes for lactate removal will also be stimulated.

Altitude training

Although many athletes from a wide range of sports including ours use altitude training regularly it is by no means certain that it will always be beneficial at low altitude. The idea of training at altitude is attractive because it holds out the possibility of enhanced oxygen capacity in the blood, although some authorities suggest that superior *anaerobic* capacity might be the result. It is usually recommended that a training camp of 3–4 weeks at an altitude of 2,000 metres should be undertaken, and that higher altitudes will do more harm than good. After such a training camp there is the possibility of improved aerobic performance for about 4–20 days after descent, i.e. after buffering capacity has been restored but before the extra haemoglobin is lost. As a general rule it would be wise to allow 10 days before a major competition. Many athletes who are used to such routines report a sense of well-being which enables them to resume their sea-level training with increased vigour after altitude, and they ascribe any better race times to this effect rather than a direct one.

Previous experience of altitude training undoubtedly helps the athlete to adjust more quickly, and it would be very unwise for any athlete to experiment with this preparation for the first time before an important competition. If the athletes are already in peak condition then the gains are likely to be small and must be weighed carefully against the possible disadvantages of training under unusual conditions. Apart from psychological problems, the disadvantages can include a reduction in training volume and intensity until acclimatization is advanced, rehearsing incorrect pace, insomnia, dry and sore throats, lower glycogen stores, dehydration and sunburn.

NUTRITION AND DIET

A good diet is essential for health and well-being and is also a prerequisite of optimum athletic performance, but such a diet is neither complex in principle nor expensive. The diet supplies the body with all the basic ingredients with which it is built and repaired, with its sources of energy, and with essential biochemicals that it cannot manufacture for itself. Even an adult's tissues are constantly being replaced and modified, and this is particularly so for the athlete in training whose tissues are responding to the stress. Such requirements for growth are of course even greater in the growing child and adolescent. Furthermore, large quantities of an enormous range of substances are used up, secreted and excreted by our bodies every day, and the losses must be made good from our diet.

There is a common fallacy that if this or that component of the diet is essential for health or sporting success then an extra large helping will lead to even better health or even greater success. Despite all the claims by those with a financial interest, there is no proven case for any boost in performance by any foodstuff, or for the vast majority of nutritional supplements, for any athlete whose diet is already adequate from normal sources. But there is the rub, how do we know if our own diet is adequate? Well, the next few pages will give you the crucial advice that you need, but we are individuals and nutrition is still not a very exact science, so it is very difficult to cater for everyone in detail. We must guard against missing out on essential ingredients, but those who are looking for a magical extra one before next Saturday will be disappointed.

Components of the diet

It is convenient to divide the essential components into seven main classes as follows:

1   Carbohydrates
2   Fats and oils
3   Proteins and amino acids
4   Vitamins
5   Minerals
6   Water
7   Roughage or fibre

Nutrition and dietetics are huge subjects by themselves and there is space here to present only an outline of the function of these seven components with special reference to our sport. For further information readers should consult more specialist texts and beware of the many crackpots and quacks who have set up home in this field.

1 Carbohydrates

Carbohydrate is the primary fuel for rowing, the major source of energy, although a number of other compounds (such as fatty acids) may make a contribution especially at low levels of effort. Carbohydrates also fulfil a huge number of other roles within our bodies, either on their own or in combination with other compounds; for example there is evidence that a good intake of carbohydrate is important for the immune system. The body has an extraordinary ability to manufacture and convert the many different types of carbohydrate that we need from the ones that we eat, but a few individuals may have some problems with this.

Carbohydrates are compounds of the elements carbon, hydrogen and oxygen only. They are conveniently classed either as sugars, such as glucose or sucrose, or polysaccharides with very much larger molecules made up from many sugar molecules, such as glycogen or starch. Enzymes in our digestive juices convert the carbohydrates to simple sugars that can be absorbed and then altered further as necessary. Most of the carbohydrate entering the blood will be glucose and is called 'blood sugar'. Excess sugar in the blood will be removed by the liver and muscles under the influence of the hormone insulin and either converted into glycogen and stored, or into fat and stored. Glycogen is readily reconverted into glucose as required. The liver stores about 100 g of glycogen and this is vital as a reserve for maintaining a constant blood glucose concentration – vital because the brain can only use glucose as its fuel. The total stored in muscle might be about 300 g in an untrained person but a fit, well-fed and rested rower may well have twice as much.

At rest less than 10% of the muscle's energy is derived from blood glucose, much of it coming from fat. During strenuous exercise however, although the rate of glucose uptake by muscle increases perhaps twenty-fold, the larger proportion is provided by muscle glycogen. As exhaustion approaches and the muscle glycogen stores become greatly depleted, the contribution of blood glucose increases. Meanwhile, the liver continues to release glucose until its stores are

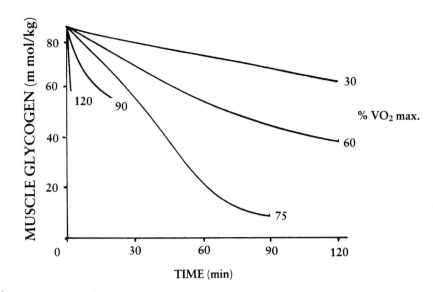

Fig. 108 The rate at which stored glycogen is used depends very much on the intensity of the exercise (after Gollnick)

nearly used up and profound exhaustion ensues involving not only the muscles but also the central nervous system. Muscle glycogen stores therefore have a great influence on endurance above 70% of aerobic capacity, which is the range of interest to us in training and competition – the larger the stores the longer the exercise can continue (fig. 108).

The mechanism for glycogen storage is activated by depletion of the reserves and by the presence of both glucose and insulin in the blood. It follows that the most rapid synthesis of muscle glycogen will occur immediately after exercise if quantities of carbohydrate are available. This effect can be exploited by eating carbohydrate-rich food or drink, particularly glucose drinks, as soon as possible after a race or training session. Such an emphasis on glycogen replenishment is important because if you are training every day, or racing frequently, your glycogen stores might not recover within 24 hours (fig. 109). Similarly, it is unwise to take in much carbohydrate in the hour before a race because this would activate glucose storage just when you want it to be released. Taking in carbohydrate immediately before or during prolonged exercise could be helpful however.

The energy value of food is measured in joules, but the value of one joule is so small that it is more usual to count them in thousands (kilojoules, kJ) or even in millions (MJ). The older units of

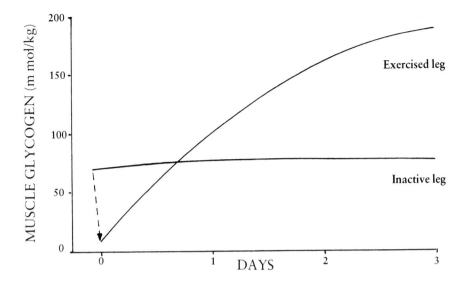

Fig. 109 Exercise severe enough to deplete the glycogen reserves substantially is the greatest stimulus to storage (after Bergstran and Hultman)

calories are still often used (one calorie equals 4.2 joules), again more usually encountered in thousands (kcal, or confusingly, Cal.). Non-scientific articles on food energy often use the word 'calories' when they actually are referring to thousands of the things. One gram of carbohydrate releases about 4 kcal = 16.8 kJ of energy, as does one gram of protein, whilst fat gives a lot more at 9 kcal = 37.8 kJ. Your personal energy requirements depend on your age, gender, size, and metabolic rate and activity level. We can be sure that your rowing and sculling training will demand a great deal of extra energy and therefore extra food compared with an inactive person. For top-class rowers or scullers training hard and regularly, it has been estimated that their daily energy requirements will be 300–315 kJ (72–75 kcal) per kilogram of body weight. For an 80 kg male this comes to 24,000–25,200 kJ (5,700–6,000 kcal) per day, and for a 70 kg female probably nearer a lower figure of 21,000 kJ (5,000 kcal).

These are very large values and will require a correspondingly large food intake to meet them. General nutritional advice now is to make carbohydrate at least 50% of the energy value of the diet, but this is not enough for our purposes. In order to meet the special energy demands of rowing and to replenish as far as possible the stocks of glycogen we should be aiming more towards 60–70%, largely through a reduction in the proportion of fat. The problem is that this does make for a rather bulky diet – 60% of 25,000 kJ would mean eating 900 g of carbohydrate a day, equivalent to fifty-five slices of bread! Even for less committed rowers, who are nevertheless training hard every day, an intake of at least 500 g of carbohydrate is necessary if they are to maintain glycogen levels and performance.

Fortunately, good carbohydrate foods are easily available and cheap, and particularly the unrefined ones with plenty of fibre which are easily digested and pass through the gut well so it is easier to cope with frequent large meals. Refined and processed foods, although rich in carbohydrates, may be rather low in other nutrients, may contain rather a lot of fat, and the sugar content may be harmful to teeth. It is now realized that as well as the desirability of avoiding these drawbacks and also making sure that we get enough of the fibre found in unrefined foods, we also need to consider the rate of digestion and absorption of the carbohydrate – what is known as the *glycaemic index*.

GLYCAEMIC INDEX

Some carbohydrates are more readily digested (if necessary) and absorbed than others and this naturally determines how quickly they appear in the bloodstream. Those that lead quickly to a rise in blood sugar are said to have a high glycaemic index, whereas the slow-release ones have a low glycaemic index. If you need a quick replenishment, say after training or a race, then carbohydrates with a high index – such as white bread, rice, potatoes (boiled or mashed without butter), rice crispies and of course, glucose – will be the thing to take. However, surges in blood sugar are taxing for the blood sugar control mechanism that relies on insulin and in the short term can affect how you feel, and in the longer term can provoke the development of type II diabetes. For other occasions then it is better to eat medium index foods (porridge, muesli, pasta, and sweet potato for example) or low ones such as chickpeas, lentils, dried apricots, fruit-yoghurt and semi-skimmed milk.

Extensive tables of glycaemic indices are available, including from your local supermarket or on the Internet and some examples are given in table 13. Some of the figures may come as a surprise because a number of other factors can affect the rate of absorption or metabolism of the food. It is not for example a simple case of high fibre foods having the lower indices – wholemeal bread has a higher index than French bread – and because fat slows digestion then crisps have a lower index than, say, baked potatoes. The amount of fat in a mixed meal will also affect the rate at which other (apparently high index) foods are absorbed, thus changing their effective index. Because sucrose (table sugar) has to be digested into its components before absorption, its index is much less than that of glucose. Fructose, which has to be changed to glucose by the liver, has an even lower index.

Table 13

Glycaemic index of some common foods

glucose	100	sucrose	65	fructose	46
Rice crispies	83	cornflakes	81	muesli	58
mashed potato	74	jacket potato	72	crisps	54
Special K	54	porridge	46	all bran	43
white bread	70	wholemeal bread	69	pitta bread	58
parsnip	68	carrots	51	peas	48
dates	72	ripe banana	58	cherries	22
baked beans	46	kidney beans	28	soya beans	20
Mars bar	65	ice cream	61	chocolate	49
hazel nuts	33	cashews	22	peanuts	22

2 Fats and oils

Fats and oils should not be regarded as villainous substances that we should do without because they clog up our arteries and cause obesity. On the contrary, some oils seem to have a protective effect on our circulatory system, and we do need at least a minimum of a wide range of types of fats and oils in our diet to maintain health and growth. These fats and oils are compounds of glycerol and fatty acids, several of which we must have in our diet somewhere because we cannot make them ourselves. Apart from their high energy value, fats are essential in many parts of our bodies for the construction of cells, and they are also necessary for the transport of fat-soluble vitamins and the manufacture of some hormones. Fat is the main energy store of the body – a 70 kg man with 10% body fat would have 63,000 calories worth, which might keep him alive for a month! That fat also acts as a shock absorber round vital organs such as the kidneys and as insulation beneath the skin.

As we have seen, fat acts as a partial source of energy for rowing, particularly at lower speeds, but for higher performance we need to emphasize the intake of carbohydrate. In Britain the average adult will eat about 100 g of fat a day, making up about 40% of the total energy, but for health reasons it is recommended that the proportion should be below 35% with particular restriction of hard animal (saturated) fats and hydrogenated oils. Reduction in body fat can have some performance benefits because of the lesser weight to be carried but it should not be overdone. Female rowers and scullers should be careful about reducing body fat too far for whatever reason because of the problem of sports amenorrhoea, and adolescent girls should never risk reaching that condition.

3 Proteins and amino acids

Proteins are very large molecules made up of a combination of simpler amino acids, of which there are twenty common forms, and as a result there is an almost infinite variety of types of protein. Every cell in our bodies contains thousands of different proteins, each with specific tasks to perform, and all of those proteins are assembled from the amino acids in our diet, or more usually from the amino acids released from proteins as we digest them. Most of us eat a great variety of proteins, unless perhaps we are following a very restricted diet, so we are likely to take in a sufficiently varied mix of amino acids for most purposes. All but seven of the amino acids can be made from others, and any excess will be broken down in the liver.

Proteins are often described as the body-building foods, but although there is much protein in the structure of cells (especially muscle cells) they have many, many other roles to fulfil. It would be wrong to assume that the intake of protein acts as a stimulus to growth, for although adequate amounts are essential there is no evidence that excess increases it. Some 40% of our body protein is found in muscle and its development depends on our genes, hormones and the training we do provided that adequate amounts of the right amino acids are available. Most of us already eat more than enough protein, and in any case it can be calculated that even if we are increasing muscle bulk through a programme of heavy weight training we only need an extra seven grams of protein a day. There is some evidence that it could be helpful to ensure good supplies of the right amino acids at or near the time of training – we could drink those amino acids, but they do taste foul! Very high mileage training may break down muscle protein and this must be replaced by extra intake – some 'recovery' sports drinks for post-exercise use contain protein and seem to work. Whey (milk) protein is particularly good.

An average daily intake of protein of about 1 g per kg body weight, and less for the less muscular female but more for the growing child, is suggested for non-athletes but this may not be enough for our purposes. It would be better to follow the other guideline of 10–15% of total energy in the daily diet. For our 80 kg athlete training hard enough to need 6,000 kcal per day this would come to about 200 g of protein. This suggests that a good mixed diet containing some high-protein foods will be fine and we don't need expensive supplements. The high carbohydrate diet that has already been proposed will minimize the use of amino acids for energy generation (very little except in starvation or exhaustion anyway), and will thus have a protein-sparing effect.

4 Vitamins

These organic chemicals are not nutrients as such because they have no energy value to us, yet they are essential in small quantities in our diet for the maintenance of health, the release of energy from food, and for growth. Tables in most nutrition books set out the functions and best sources of the principal vitamins, and the (frequently revised) suggested intakes of them. These latter figures vary greatly from one authority to another, but the truth of the matter is that very little is known for sure about the amounts we need because it is difficult to do fully controlled experiments on humans. Because these substances are clearly very important in exercise it is tempting to believe that we must take in more, either in hope that they will boost performance or just as insurance. There is some scientific evidence for this, particularly for some of the energy-releasing B vitamins and C. These water soluble vitamins can be safely tolerated in higher than normal doses but we must be cautious because, for example, recent research indicates that large intakes of anti-oxidants can be harmful and the fat soluble vitamins A and D have long been known to be toxic in excess. A good mixed diet with plenty of fresh ingredients (not overcooked) along with not too much that is refined or processed, and following the recommendation to include at least five portions of fruit or vegetables a day, is almost bound to provide enough of all the vitamins. If there is any ground for concern then a small supplement is unlikely to do any harm.

5 Minerals

These inorganic substances (in solution as charged particles called ions, hence *electrolytes*) are present in our body fluids and cells in a range of concentrations where they fulfil a wide variety of functions. For best functioning these concentrations should remain more or less constant, a task that is largely accomplished by our kidneys.

Because minerals are regularly used up and only stored to a limited extent, as well as excreted in sweat and urine, they must be replaced through the diet. There is no doubt that the active athlete will have to increase intake of some of them to match the more rapid losses. As with vitamins, however, there is no evidence that excessive intake will improve performance and in some cases it is likely to be harmful. Again, a good mixed diet of quality foods in adequate energy amounts should take care of our needs without supplementation. We do need to take particular care to ensure that we make up for sweat losses of sodium and potassium, and that we get enough iron from easily used sources such as meat – iron is a key component of haemoglobin and also used in energy release, but a surprising proportion of athletes may be anaemic. If you are on any sort of restricted diet you may need supplementation and women (especially young ones or any suffering heavy menstrual bleeding) may need extra iron. Sports drinks usually contain good mixtures of electrolytes to help replace sweat losses and these are very valuable but some of the other ingredients (such as vitamins) may not be. In general our food contains enough salt and too much may lead to undesirable increases in blood pressure.

6 Water

The importance of adequate water supplies in hot weather has already been stressed earlier in this chapter, but even in more normal conditions we will need two litres or more per day. Many of us probably do not drink enough water and it would be better to err a bit on the generous side (but not too much because of the danger of diluting our body fluids and causing tissue swelling), and let our kidneys deal with the excess rather than risk dehydration. As mentioned before, pale and copious urine is a good sign, but thirst is not as it shows that we are already dehydrated. Intriguingly, some early books on rowing and other athletic training clung to the belief that severe restriction of fluid intake was an essential part of fitness training. Such methods must have been uncomfortable, ineffective and highly dangerous at times.

Plain water in moderate amounts will be fine for maintaining hydration but drinks containing carbohydrate and salt will be better in prolonged training, very long races, and for recovery. Commercial sports drinks are not necessary and a much cheaper alternative would be diluted glucose, Ribena or fruit juice, plus a pinch of salt (0.1% per litre). The sugar content will help to replace that used by the muscles and concentrations of up to 5% can be emptied from the stomach as rapidly as water. When combined with a little salt the rate of absorption of both glucose and water in the intenstine will be enhanced. Many commercially available drinks are more concentrated than this and 6% or more of glucose is more suited to post-exercise replenishment. Glucose seems to be the best sugar to use, as polymers are more expensive and offer no clear benefit, whilst fructose (in fruit juices for example) is not so well absorbed, can cause gut trouble and may harm performance. Drinking large amounts of plain water to make up for sweat losses is potentially dangerous because it can dilute the remaining sodium in the blood (hyponatraemia).

Drinks containing caffeine (coffee, tea, Coca-Cola) will not infringe the doping regulations but are often thought to be diuretic. However, recent research shows clearly that they do not cause water loss, so these can safely be part of your fluid intake. Alcohol, though, is quite definitely contra-indicated, and because of its other effects should be avoided for at least 48 hours before an event.

7 Roughage or dietary fibre

Plant fibres that we cannot digest give a firmer bulk to our food as it passes through our gut, and this helps the muscular action that transports it and finally eliminates it. Adequate fibre helps to prevent constipation and some diseases of the large intestine, and some types also seem to help the circulatory system. As with other things, excess can be harmful. If you regularly eat fruit and vegetables, as I recommended earlier, then you should have plenty of fibre and there will be no need to look for any more.

Losing weight

If you follow the training and dietary advice given earlier you will probably lose body fat and look leaner, but you may not lose weight because some of the weight of the fat will have been replaced by muscle and connective tissue. If further fat losses are desired then you could restrict calorie intake a little but you need to beware of reducing training and racing capability, and you might find it hard to maintain. It would be better to emphasize low fat intake but to maintain good carbohydrate and protein quantities. There is emerging evidence that high protein proportions help to restrict appetite, but low carbohydrate diets such as *Zone* or *Atkins* are not advisable for athletes in our sport. It is not true, by the way, that when you stop training the muscle will turn to fat, but you may find it difficult to reduce your food intake to take account of your smaller energy needs.

Fit adult male rowers will probably have about 10% body fat and females will be more likely to be in the range 15–20%; lightweights on the other hand will often be well below this, even as low as 3.5% – but any less than this is regarded as harmful. Lightweights will have to be careful with both the composition and quantity of their meals but should never use starvation and severe dehydration as a way to make the weight. They should aim to maintain target weight, or a little less, well before competition so that they can continue to eat and drink sensibly in the last few days. It is common practice to lose the last pound or two in a pre-weigh-in outing, and there is no harm in this because the lost fluid can be made up before the race.

HYGIENE AND BLISTERS

Skin damage and infections are uncomfortable and deleterious to performance and it is worth taking some precautions. Keep your skin and kit clean and always shower or bath after training or racing. If the skin does get damaged then clean it thoroughly and cover it with a sterile and frequently changed dressing. Small blisters are best left alone and with some protection will go away and leave the skin tougher. Larger blisters are likely to burst next outing anyway and should be emptied by piercing with a *sterile* needle, leaving the skin intact to be covered and protected. Savlon has been found to be very useful because it is not only antiseptic but it seems to help skin healing, and will keep damaged areas supple and lessen the risk of cracking. Protecting the damaged hands just with sticking plasters is not always successful because they come off, and a better answer may be to cover them with a light cotton glove or cycle mitt. With use the skin of the hands will thicken and harden and this can be encouraged in advance of the rowing season by twisting a piece of smooth wood between the hands. There is no doubt that a loose hold of the handle and good feathering technique will help to minimize blisters.

RECAPITULATION

Looking after yourself so that you are not harmed, or your performance reduced by avoidable factors is only common sense, and now that you are armed with the information in this chapter you can take the necessary practical steps. This book is largely devoted to ways of improving your performance – by increasing your skill, by improving your training for strength and endurance, and by helping you to get the most out of your boat and out of yourself in racing. It would be tragic to fail to make the most of it or to waste what you have gained by neglecting your health or by taking in an inadequate diet.

Making a success in rowing or sculling has been likened to making a cake – you need all the right ingredients in all the right proportions, and cooked in just the right way for the correct length of time. I hope that what you have read here will help you to select the right mix for you to achieve your ambitions in the sport. As a famous coach once said to me, 'if you do this you may not be world champion, but you won't be bad!'

Index